Child Protection

Fergus Smith
B.Sc.(Hons), M.A., C.Q.S.W., D.M.S., Dip.M

Edina Carmi
B.Sc.(Hons), Dip.App. Soc. Studies, C.Q.S.W. C.S.S.M

Children Act Enterprises Ltd
Pantiles Langham Road
Robertsbridge
East Sussex TN32 5EP
tel: 01580 880243

www.caeuk.org

© Fergus Smith 2010

British Library Cataloguing in Publication Data
A catalogue record for this book is available from the
British Library

ISBN 978 1 899986 18 7

Designed and typeset by Helen Joubert Design
Printed in the UK by The Lavenham Press

CAE is an independent organisation which publishes
guides to family and criminal law and provides
consultancy, research, training and independent
investigation services to the public, private and voluntary
sectors.

Contents

In exercising social services functions, local authorities are required to act under the general guidance of the Secretary of State (s.7(1) Local Authority Social Services Act 1970). In R v Islington LBC, ex parte Ritson (1996) 32 BMLR 136 at 140 Sedley J described the effect of s.7(1): ' in my view Parliament, by s.7(1), has required local authorities to follow the path charted by the Secretary of State's guidance, with liberty to deviate from it where the local authority judges , on admissible grounds, that there is good reason to do so, but without freedom to take a substantially different course'

This direction has since been followed in R v Lambeth LBC ex p K [2000] 3 CCLR 141 and in R (on the application of AB and SB) v Nottingham City Council [2001] 3 FCR 350

The text of this guide reflects statutory and the most significant case law available as at June 2010

Introduction

■ This guide is for those in England and Wales * who provide or support safeguarding services. It offers a simple, accurate summary and reinforces understanding of current law and government guidance.

■ It is designed for rapid reference by:

  • Doctors, nurses and other health professionals
  • Social workers
  • Police and probation officers
  • Education staff
  • Others in statutory and independent settings who suspect a child is being abused or neglected

■ The guide should be used only to supplement, not replace information derived from national or local guidance, procedures and legal advice.

■ Appendix 1 summarises current law about consent and refusal by children of assessment or treatment and appendix 2, current requirements and professional expectations of doctors with respect to confidentiality and contraception for those aged less than 16 years old.

  Wales has comparable legislation to England. The National Assembly for Wales published its statutory guidance in 2006. References in this guide to numbered paras. are to the latest English 'Working Together to Safeguard Children' published in March 2010.

Definitions [arranged alphabetically]

Care Plan [s.31A CA 1989 as inserted by s.121 ACA 2002]

■ When an application is made which might result in a Care Order, the appropriate local authority (the one proposed to be designated in the order) must, within a time-scale directed by the court prepare a 'care plan' (referred to in the ACA 2002 as a 's.31A plan') for the future care of the child.

■ While the application is pending, the local authority must keep the plan under review and revise or replace it if this is required.

NB. A care plan must give any prescribed information and do so in the prescribed manner.

Child [s.105 (1) CA 1989]

■ For the purposes of child protection, a 'child' is a person of less than 18 years of age.

'Child in Need' [s.17 (10); (11) CA 1989]

■ A child is 'in need' if:

   • S/he is unlikely to achieve or maintain, or have the opportunity to so do, a reasonable standard of health or development without provision of services by a local authority, or if

- Her/his health or development is likely to be significantly impaired, or further impaired, without such services, or
- S/he is disabled

NB. Health = physical or mental; Development = physical, intellectual, emotional, social or behavioural; Disabled = blind, deaf, dumb or suffering from mental disorder of any kind or substantially and permanently handicapped by illness, injury or congenital deformity, or other such disability as may be prescribed.

■ Each local authority has a general duty to safeguard and promote welfare of children in need in its area, and so far as is consistent with that duty, promote their upbringing by their families by providing a range and level of services appropriate to their needs [s.17 (1) CA 1989].

NB. A child who is at risk of 'significant harm' (see below) may be assumed to be a child in need and therefore eligible for family support services.

■ Such children include those in Young Offender Institutions (YOIs) and in young persons' wings of prisons. Prison Service Instruction (PSI) 28/2009 (applicable from 19.10.09 to 08.10.12) details the requirements of Governors/Directors of such establishments.

Child Protection Plan

■ The 'core group' (see below) is responsible for developing the 'outline child protection plan' agreed at an initial child protection conference into a 'child protection plan' which sets out what work needs to be done, why, when and by whom.

■ The overall aim of the plan is to:

- Ensure the child is safe and prevent her/him from suffering further harm by supporting the strengths, addressing the vulnerabilities and risk factors and helping meet the child's unmet needs
- Promote the child's health and development i.e. welfare and
- Provided it is in her/his best interests, support the family and wider family members to safeguard and promote the welfare of their child

■ The full child protection plan should:

- Describe the identified developmental needs of the child and what therapeutic services are required
- Include specific, achievable, child-focused outcomes intended to safeguard and promote her/his welfare
- Include realistic strategies and specific actions to achieve planned outcomes
- Set out when and in what situations the child will be seen by the lead social worker, both alone and with other family members or caregivers present

- Clearly identify roles and responsibilities of professionals and family members, including those with routine contact with the child e.g. health visitors, GPs and teachers and the nature and frequency of contact by those professionals with child and family members
- Include a contingency plan to be followed if circumstances change significantly and require prompt action, including initiating family court proceedings to safeguard and promote the child's welfare
- Lay down points at which progress will be reviewed and the means by which progress will be judged

■ The plan should also:

- Take into account the wishes and feelings of the child and of the parent/s insofar as they are consistent with the child's welfare
- Be explained to the family via the lead social worker so that they understand the required outcomes and accept and are willing to work to the plan
- Be provided in the family's preferred language

■ If families' preferences are not accepted, reasons should be provided and they should be told of their right to complain or make representations and how to do so.

Children's Services Authority (CSA)

- A CSA in England is defined by s.65 CA 2004 as a:

  - County council
  - Metropolitan district council
  - Non metropolitan district council for an area where there is no county council i.e. a unitary
  - A London borough council
  - The Common Council of the City of London and
  - The Isles of Scilly

- A CSA in Wales is defined also in s.65, as a:

  - County council or
  - County borough council

Common Assessment Framework (CAF)

- The CAF is a tool to enable early and effective assessment of children and young people who need additional services or support from more than one agency.

- CAF is a holistic consent-based assessment framework which records, in a single place and in a structured and consistent way, every aspect of a child's life, family and environment.

- National eCAF which is still being developed will be a secure IT system for storing and accessing information captured through the CAF process.

  NB. Children's Trust Boards should have clear arrangements in place for local implementation of

CAF. A CAF is not a referral form though it may be used to support a referral or a specialist assessment.

Core Assessment [Para.3.11 Framework for the Assessment of Children in Need & Their Families]

■ An in-depth assessment which addresses the central or most important aspects of the needs of a child and the capacity of her/his parents or caregivers to respond appropriately to those needs within the wider family and community context.

NB. Though led by Children's Social Care, such assessments (which should be completed within 35 working days) will invariably involve other agencies or independent professionals).

Core Group

■ The core group is responsible for developing the outline protection plan into a full child protection plan that can be used as a working tool.

■ Membership should include the lead social worker who chairs the core group, the child if appropriate, family members and professionals/foster carers who will have direct contact with the family.

■ Although the lead social worker has lead responsibility, for the formulation and implementation of the child protection plan, all members are jointly responsible for carrying out these tasks, refining the plan as needed and monitoring progress against planned outcomes.

- Agencies should ensure that members of the core group undertake their roles and responsibilities effectively in accordance with the agreed child protection plan.

- The first meeting of the core group should take place within 10 working days of an initial protection conference.

- The first core group meeting is to flesh out the protection plan and decide what steps need to be taken by whom to complete the core assessment on time.

- Thereafter, core groups should meet sufficiently regularly to facilitate working together, monitor actions and outcomes against the protection plan and make any necessary alterations as circumstances change.

  NB. The lead social worker should ensure a record of decisions taken and actions agreed at core groups as well as of the written views of those unable to attend. The child protection plan should be updated as necessary.

'Designated' Professional

- All PCTs should have a 'designated' doctor and nurse who have a strategic, professional lead on all aspects of the health service contribution to safeguarding children (including all providers) across the PCT area.

■ The designated professional role should always be
explicitly defined in job descriptions and sufficient
time and funding allowed to fulfil it effectively.

■ The designated professional should provide advice
and support to named professionals in each provider
Trust and s/he is a vital source of professional advice
to other professionals, PCT, local authority and to the
LSCB.

*NB. 'Safeguarding Children and Young People: Roles
and Competencies for Health Care Staff which is
currently being updated can be accessed via www.
rcpch.ac.uk/doc.aspx?id_Resource=1535*

Emotional Abuse

■ Emotional abuse is the persistent emotional ill
treatment of a child such as to cause severe and
persistent effects on the child's emotional
development.

■ It may involve conveying to children that they are
worthless or unloved, inadequate, or valued only
insofar as they meet the needs of another person.

■ It may include not giving the child opportunities to
express views, deliberately silencing her/him or
'making fun' of what s/he says or how s/he
communicates.

■ It may feature age or developmentally inappropriate
expectations being imposed on a child, including
interactions that are beyond the child's capability as

well as overprotection and limitation of exploration and learning, or preventing her/him participating in normal social interaction.

- Emotional abuse may involve seeing or hearing the ill-treatment of another person, involve serious bullying (including cyber-bullying) causing children to feel frightened or in danger or the exploitation or corruption of children.

- Some level of emotional abuse is involved in all types of ill treatment of children, though emotional abuse may occur alone.

Lead Member

- The lead Member for Children's Services has delegated responsibility from the Council for children, young people and their families and is politically accountable for ensuring that the local authority fulfils its legal responsibilities for safeguarding and promoting the welfare of children and young people.

- The lead Member should provide the political leadership needed for the effective co-ordination of work with other relevant agencies that have safeguarding responsibilities e.g. Police, and Health Services.

- The lead Member should also take steps to assure her/himself that effective quality assurance systems for safeguarding are in place and functioning effectively.

Lead Social Worker

- The lead social worker (a General Social Care Council –registered social worker from Children's Social Care or NSPCC) is responsible for making sure that the outline child protection plan is developed into a more detailed inter-agency plan and has the lead role in inter-agency work with the family.

- S/he should complete the core assessment of child/ family securing contributions from core group members and other as necessary and review progress against the agreed objectives.

- The lead social worker is also responsible for acting as the lead professional for inter-agency work with child and family.

  NB. This role should be fully explained at the initial child protection conference and at the core group.

Local Authority [s.105 CA 1989]

- The term 'local authority' in the Children Act 1989 means a county council, metropolitan district, London borough or a unitary authority, not just Children's Social Care.

Looked After Child [s.22 CA 1989]

- Children 'looked after' by a local authority may be 'accommodated', 'in care' or 'remanded/detained'.

- Accommodation is a voluntary arrangement in which the local authority does not gain parental

responsibility and no notice is required for removal of
the child.

■ 'In care' means that a court has made a child subject
of a Care Order which gives the local authority
parental responsibility and (some) authority to limit
parents' exercise of their continuing parental
responsibility.

■ A local authority is authorised to detain those in the
third category who may acquire such status as a
result of:

• Remand by a court following criminal charges
• Detention following arrest by police
• An Emergency Protection Order (which also
awards temporary parental responsibility to the
local authority) or Child Assessment Order
• A 'criminal' Supervision Order with a residence
requirement

Named Professional

■ All NHS (including Foundation) Trusts, public, third
sector, independent sector, social enterprises and
PCTs providing services for children should identify a
'named' doctor and a named nurse/midwife for

safeguarding. In the case of NHS Direct, Ambulance Trusts and independent providers, this should be a named professional.

■ The focus for such a named professional is safeguarding children within the organisation. S/he has a key role in promoting good professional practice within the agency and providing advice and expertise for colleagues.

■ The named professional should work closely with the safeguarding children board lead to ensure that all services are aware of their responsibilities.

■ The named professional is usually responsible for:

• Conducting the organisation's internal management reviews (IMRs) (unless personal involvement makes it more appropriate for the designated professional to conduct the exercise)
• Ensuring actions plans emerging from serious case reviews (SCRs) are followed up

Neglect

■ Neglect is the persistent failure to meet a child's basic physical and/or psychological needs, likely to result in the serious impairment of her/his health and development.

■ Neglect may occur during pregnancy as a result of maternal substance abuse.

■ Neglect may involve a parent or carer failing to:

- Provide adequate food and clothing
- Provide shelter e.g. exclusion from home or abandonment
- Protect a child from physical and emotional harm or danger or
- Ensure adequate supervision including use of inadequate care takers or
- Ensure access to appropriate medical care/ treatment, and may also include neglect of child's basic emotional needs).

■ Evidence of neglect is built up over time and can cover a range of parenting tasks.

Outline Child Protection Plan

■ Following a decision made at an initial or review conference to register or continue registration/that a child does need or continues to need a protection plan, an 'outline child protection plan' should:

- Identify risk and protective factors based upon current findings from the assessment and information held from any previous involvement with child and family
- Establish short and long-term aims and objectives that are clearly linked to reducing the likelihood of harm to the child and promoting her/his welfare, including contact with family members
- Be clear about who will have responsibility for what actions – including actions by family members – within what timescales

- Outline ways of monitoring and evaluating progress against planned outcomes set out in the plan
- Be clear about which professional is responsible for checking that the required changes have taken place and what action will be taken, by whom when they have not

Paramountcy Principle [s.1 (1) CA 1989]

■ When a court determines any question with respect to a child's upbringing, administration of property or income, the child's welfare must be the paramount consideration.

■ The House of Lords has confirmed that where both parent and child are 'children' within the meaning of the Act, the needs of the younger (non-parent) child are paramount [Birmingham City Council v H (NO.2) 1 FLR 883 1993].

Parental Responsibility [s.3 CA 1989]

■ 'Parental responsibility' means all the rights, duties, powers, responsibilities and authority which by law a parent has in relation to a child and her/his property.

■ Where a child's parents were married to each other at any time following her/his conception they each have parental responsibility for the child [s.2 (1) CA 1989 & s.1 FLRA 1987].

- If a married couple separate or divorce, they both continue to have parental responsibility for their child/ren.

  NB. Similarly, a couple in a registered civil partnership who have parental responsibility and who subsequently separate or dissolve the partnership would both retain their parental responsibility.

- Parental responsibility can be lost only if a child is freed for adoption, adopted, a court so orders, s/he attains the age of 18 or s/he dies.

- Each parent/other person with parental responsibility can act independently in the exercise of it e.g. giving consent to medical treatment.

- Where a child's mother and father were not married to each other at any time following her/his conception, the:

  - Mother has parental responsibility for the child [s.2(2) (a) CA 1989] and
  - Father will have parental responsibility if he has acquired it and not ceased to have it [s.2(2) (b) CA 1989 as amended by s.111 ACA 2002]]

- s.4 CA 1989 has been amended by s.111 (1) – (3) ACA 2002 to allow an unmarried father to obtain parental responsibility, if:

  - He registers as the child's father in England and Wales under specified sections of the Births and Deaths Registration Act 1953 (or their equivalents in Scotland and Northern Ireland) [s.111(2)(a) ACA 2002]

- He and the child's mother make a 'parental responsibility agreement' providing for him to have parental responsibility for the child [s.111(2)(b) ACA 2002] or

- The court, on his application, orders that he shall have parental responsibility for the child [s.111(2)(c) ACA 2002]

NB. An unmarried father could also acquire parental responsibility if the child's mother had appointed him in her will as the child's guardian, and subsequently died [s.5 (6) CA 1989].

■ A step-parent (who is married to, or a civil partner of a child's mother) can obtain parental responsibility via a parental responsibility agreement or order.

NB. Ed.6 of CAE's guide to the Children Act 1989 in the context of the Human Rights Act 1998 provides further detail about allocation and acquisition of parental responsibility.

■ The essence of parental responsibility is that it is a status not merely a set of rights, duties and powers [Re S (Parental Responsibility) [1995] 2 FLR 648].

■ The *practical* advantages of such a status include:

- A right to receive educational reports and provide consent to school trips

- A right to consent to treatment for, and receive medical reports about the child

- An ability to sign official papers e.g. passport application
- An ability to prevent a child's mother removing her/him from the UK
- A right to object to a proposed change of name
- A right to object to a child being accommodated by a local authority and an ability to lawfully remove her/him
- Being regarded as a 'parent' for purposes of adoption proceedings

NB. In order to comply with Article 8(1) of the European Convention, best practice is to treat the unmarried father who does not have parental responsibility as possessing full rights. [See CAE's companion guide to the 'Children Act 1989 in the Context of the Human Rights Act 1998' for comprehensive coverage of the significance of the European Convention for work with children and families].

Physical Abuse

■ Physical abuse may involve hitting, shaking, throwing, poisoning, burning or scalding, drowning, suffocating or otherwise causing physical harm to a child.

■ Physical harm may also be caused when a parent or carer feigns symptoms of, or deliberately causes, ill-health to a child (variously described as 'fabricated or induced illness' see p.121)

Record that Child is Subject of a Child Protection Plan

- Children's Social Care IT systems should be capable of capturing in the child's case record whether s/he is subject of a child protection plan.

- Each local authority IT system which is supporting the Integrated Children's System (ICS) should be capable of producing a list of all children resident in the area (including any placed there by another local authority) who are considered to be at continuing risk of significant harm, and for whom there is a child protection plan.

- The main purpose of having the above capacity is to enable agencies and professionals to be aware of those children assessed to be at continuing risk of significant harm and who are subject of a child protection plan.

- Police and health professionals must be able to access the above information in and out of office hours.

Sexual Abuse

- Sexual abuse involves forcing or enticing a child or young person to take part in sexual activities, including prostitution whether or not s/he is aware of what is happening.

- Activities may involve physical contact, including penetrative (e.g. rape or oral sex) or non-penetrative acts such as masturbation, kissing, rubbing and touching outside of clothing.

■ Sexual abuse may take non-contact activities e.g. involving a child in looking at, or in production of pornography, watching sexual activities or encouraging her/him to behave in sexually inappropriate ways or grooming a child in preparation for abuse (including via the internet).

NB. Sexual abuse in not solely perpetrated by adult males. Women and children can also commit acts of sexual abuse.

Sex Offender Register

■ The notification requirements of Part 2 of the Sexual Offences Act 2003 (the sex offenders register) are an automatic requirement on offenders who receive a conviction or caution for certain sexual offences.

■ The notification requirements are intended to ensure that the police are informed of the whereabouts of offenders in the community.

■ Offenders must notify police of certain personal details within 3 days of conviction or caution for relevant sexual offences (or if in prison on that date, within 3 days of release).

■ Such an offender must then notify police within 3 days of any change to the notified details and whenever s/he spends 7 days or more at another address. All offenders must re-confirm their details at least once every 12 months and notify police 7 days in advance of any travel overseas lasting 3 days or more.

■ The period of time that an offender must comply with these requirements depends on whether they received a conviction or a caution and, where appropriate, the sentence received.

■ Notification requirements do not bar offenders from certain types of employment or from being alone with children.

NB. Failure to comply with these requirements is a criminal offence and the police should be contacted if such an offence is committed.

Significant Harm [s.31 (9) CA 1989 as amended by s.120 ACA 2002]

■ 'Significant harm' is the threshold which justifies compulsory intervention in family life.

■ Harm means ill-treatment or impairment of health or development (including impairment suffered from seeing or hearing ill-treatment of another introduced by s.120 ACA 2002).

■ Development means physical, intellectual, emotional, social or behavioural development and health means physical or mental health. Ill-treatment includes sexual abuse and forms of ill-treatment which are not physical.

■ Where the question of whether harm suffered by a
child is significant turns on the child's health and
development, her/his health or development must be
compared with that which could reasonably be
expected of a similar child [s.31(10) CA 1989].

Welfare Checklist [s.1 (3) CA 1989]

■ In considering an opposed s.8 Order or Care or
Supervision Order (including Interim Care and
Supervision and Education Supervision Orders), the
court must have regard to checklist of:

- Child's wishes/feelings
- Physical, emotional, educational needs
- Likely effect of change of circumstances
- Age, sex, background, relevant characteristics
  (this should include race, culture, religion and
  language)
- Actual or potential harm
- Capability of parents/relevant others to meet
  child's needs
- Available range of powers

AGENCY RESPONSIBILITIES

Statutory Safeguarding Duties

- The following organisations have a duty under s.11 Children Act 2004 to 'ensure that their functions are discharged with regard to the need to safeguard and promote the welfare of children':

  - County level local authorities
  - Unitary local authorities
  - District councils
  - NHS Bodies – Strategic Health Authorities, designated Special Health Authorities, Primary Care Trusts, NHS and NHS Foundation Trusts
  - Police (including British Transport Police)
  - Probation and Prisons under the National Offender Management structure
  - Youth Offending Teams
  - Secure Training Centres
  - Connexions
  - Any person to the extent s/he is providing services in pursuance of s.74 Education and Skills Act 2008

- Guidance is contained in '*Making Arrangements to Safeguard and Promote the Welfare of Children*' HM Government 2007 see www.everychildmatters.gov. uk/resources-and-practice/IG00042/

- The critical roles of police, health and education services are covered in detail on pages 26 – 46 of this guide.

■ Other agencies with statutory responsibilities for safeguarding and promoting the welfare of children are:

- Early years providers under s.40 Childcare Act 2006 in complying with welfare requirements of the Early Years Foundation Stage
- The Children and Family Courts Advisory and Support Service (CAFCASS) under s.12(1) Criminal Justice and Court Services Act 2000
- The United Kingdom Border Agency (UKBA) under s.55 Borders, Citizenship and Immigration Act 2009

NB. The UKBA instructions 'Arrangements to Safeguard and Promote Children's Welfare in the UK Border Agency may be found at www.ukba. homeoffice.gov.uk/sitecontent/documents/ policyandlaw/legislation/bci-act1/

■ All organisations must have in place safe recruitment policies and practices including enhanced Criminal Record Bureau (CRB) checks for all staff, including agency staff, students and volunteers working with children. It is an offence knowingly to employ a person 'barred' by the Independent Safeguarding Authority (ISA) from working in posts that involve caring for or treating children.

NB. CAE's guide to the Safeguarding Vulnerable Groups Act 2006 provides detailed explanation of how the vetting and barring system is supposed to operate.

Common Features of All Agencies

■ So as to fulfil their commitment to safeguard and
promote the welfare of children, *all* organisations
that provide services for children, or work with
children need to have in place:

- Clear priorities for safeguarding and promoting
the welfare of children explicitly stated in
strategic policy documents

- A clear commitment by senior management to
the importance of safeguarding and promoting
children's welfare

- A clear line of accountability within the
organisation for work on safeguarding and
promoting the welfare of children

- Recruitment and human resources management
procedures that take account of the need to
protect children and young people including
arrangements for appropriate checks on new
staff and volunteers

- Procedures for dealing with allegations of abuse
against members of staff and volunteers

- Arrangements to ensure all staff undertake
appropriate training to equip them to carry out
their responsibilities effectively, and keep this up
to date by regular refresher training and that all
staff, including temporary staff and volunteers
who work with children, are made aware of the
establishment's arrangements for safeguarding

Police

- The main roles of the Police are to uphold the law, prevent crime and disorder and protect the citizen.

- All Forces have child abuse investigation units (CAIUs), and normally take primary responsibility for investigating child abuse cases.

- All CAIUs have IT capacity under the national IMPACT Nominal Index (INI) to quickly check which Forces hold information on a particular individual. The INI's capacity draws data from a number of police databases including child protection, domestic violence, crime, custody and intelligence. Police Forces are in the process of migrating to the Police National Database (PND) which will continue and enhance this facility.

- *'Investigating Child Abuse and Safeguarding Children'* ed. 2 was published by the Association of Chief Police Officers (ACPO) and the National Police Improvement Agency in 2009. It sets out the suggested investigative doctrine, and terms of reference, for CAIUs.

- Safeguarding children is not solely the role of CAIU officers and is a fundamental part of the duties of all officers, reflecting the Children Act 2004 duty on the Force to 'safeguard and promote the welfare of children'.

■ Officers engaged in, e.g. crime and disorder reduction partnerships, drug action teams etc. must keep in mind the needs of children in their area and patrol officers attending domestic violence incidents, should be aware of the effect of such violence on any children normally resident within the household

■ Police hold important information about children who may be at risk of harm as well as those who cause such harm and should share this information and intelligence with other organisations where this is necessary to protect children.

■ The above requirement includes a responsibility to ensure that those officers representing the Force at a child protection conference are fully informed about the case as well as being experienced in risk assessment and the decision-making process. Other organisations should share with them information and intelligence they hold to enable the police to carry out their duties.

■ Police are responsible for evidence gathering in criminal investigations. This task can be carried out in conjunction with other agencies but the police are ultimately accountable for the product of criminal enquiries.

■ Police should be notified as soon as possible by Children's Social Care if a criminal offence has been committed, or is suspected of having been committed, against a child.

■ Receipt of such notification does not mean that in all cases a full investigation will be required, or that there will necessarily be any further Police involvement. It is important that police retain the opportunity to be informed and consulted, so as to ensure all relevant information can be taken into account before a final decision is made.

Health Services

General Principles

■ Health professionals have a key role to play in actively promoting the health and well-being of children and all those who work directly with them need to ensure that safeguarding and promoting their welfare forms an integral part of the care they offer.

■ Other health professionals who come into contact with children, parents and carers in the course of their work- also need to be aware of their responsibility to safeguard and promote the welfare of children.

■ All health professionals who work with children and families should be able to:

  • Understand the risk factors and recognise children in need of support and/or safeguarding
  • Recognise the needs of parents who may need extra help in bringing up their children ands know where to refer for help and use the CAF to access support as appropriate for them
  • Recognise the risks of abuse to an unborn child
  • Communicate effectively with children and young people and stay focused on the child's safety and welfare
  • Liaise closely with other agencies including health professionals and share information as appropriate

- Assess the needs of children and the capacity of parents/carers to meet their children's needs including the needs of those who display sexually harmful behaviours
- Plan and respond to the needs of children and families, particularly those who are vulnerable
- Contribute to child protection conferences, family group conferences and strategy discussions
- Contribute to planning support for children at risk of significant harm e.g. those living in households with domestic violence, parental substance misuse
- Help ensure that children who have been abused and parents under stress e.g. who have mental health problems, have access to supportive services
- Help ensure that children who have been abused or neglected and parents under stress have access to services to support them
- Be alert to the strong links between adult domestic violence and substance misuse and child abuse and recognise when a child is in need of help, services or at potential risk of suffering significant harm
- When appropriate, play an active part, through the child protection plan in keeping the child safe
- As part of generally safeguarding children, provide ongoing promotional and preventative support through proactive work with children, families and expectant parents

- Contribute to child death and serious case reviews and implementation of lessons learned

■ The above should be undertaken with reference to the core processes set out in *Working Together* 2010 and summarised in '*What to do if you're worried a child is being abused*; *Responding to domestic abuse: a handbook for health professionals*' at www.dh.gov.uk/prod_consum_dh/groups/dh_digitalassets/@dh/@en/documents/digitalasset/dh_4126619.pdf ; *Improving safety, Reducing Harm: Children, young people and domestic violence*: a practical toolkit for front line practitioners www.dh.gov.uk/en/Publicationsandstatistics/Publications/PublicationsPolicyAndGuidance/DH_108697 as well as LSCB procedures.

■ It is essential that all health professionals and their teams have access to advice and support from named and designated child safeguarding professionals, clinical supervisions and undertake regular safeguarding training and updating.

Health Organisations

Care Quality Commission (CQC)

■ The CQC is the independent regulator of safety and quality for all health services. From April 2010 NHS Trusts and NHS Foundations Trusts have had to be registered with the CQC.

■ GP practices and high street dental practices will be required to register with the CQC whether they provide wholly private or wholly NHS services or a mixture of both, and will be subject to a consistent set of quality standards.

NB. Registration of primary dental care providers will begin from 2011 and primary medical care providers from 2012.

■ NHS Foundation Trusts are accountable to an independent corporate body called 'Monitor' which is responsible for authorising, monitoring and regulating them. NHS Trusts are overseen by Strategic Health Authorities (see below).

Strategic Health Authority (SHA)

■ SHAs should consider individual organisations' arrangements for and contribution to, safeguarding children as an integral part of their governance system. Their performance and management of the health are system should be informed by information such as existing national data collections, LSCB audit, progress against action plans and/or child death and serious case review recommendations and regulatory/inspection findings.

■ SHA membership of LSCBs (see pp.53) enable them to oversee the health contribution to safeguarding children at a local level.

Primary Care Trust Commissioners (PCTs)

■ PCTs are responsible for improving the health and well being of their local population, including children and young people. They are under a duty to make arrangements to ensure that in discharging their functions, they have regard to the need to safeguard and promote the welfare of children.

■ PCTs should:

- Work with local authorities to commission and provide co-ordinated, and where possible, integrated services
- Identify a lead officer for children and young people to ensure their needs are at the forefront of local planning and service delivery (National Standards Framework NSF Core Standard 3- Markers of good practice)

■ PCT chief executives have responsibility for ensuring that the health contribution to safeguarding and promoting the welfare of children is discharged effectively across the whole local health economy through the PCT's commissioning arrangements.

■ PCTs must co-operate with the local authority in the establishment and operation of the LSCB and as partners share responsibility for the effective discharge of its functions. Representation on the Board should be at an appropriate level of seniority.

■ PCTs are also responsible for providing and/or ensuring the availability of appropriate expertise and advice and support to the LSCBs in respect of a range of specialist health functions e.g. primary care, mental health (adult and child and adolescent) and sexual health, and for co-ordinating the health component of serious case reviews

- The PCT must also ensure that all health organisations including the independent health care sector with whom it has commissioning arrangements, have links with a specific LSCB and that health agencies work in partnership in accordance with their agreed LSCB plan (this is particularly important where Trusts' boundaries/ catchment areas straddle those of LSCBs).

- PCTs should ensure all health providers from whom they commission services- both public and independent sector- have comprehensive single and multi-agency policies and procedures to safeguard and promote the welfare of children which are in line with and informed by LSCB procedures, and are easily accessible for staff at all levels within each organisation.

- Each PCT is responsible for identifying a senior paediatrician, and senior nurse to undertake the role of 'designated' professionals for child protection across the health economy and for identifying a 'named' doctor and a named nurse (or midwife) who will take a professional lead within the PCT on child protection matters.

- PCTs should ensure that all their staff:

- Are alert to the need to safeguard and promote the welfare of children
- Have knowledge of local procedures and
- Know how to contact the named and designated professionals

■ PCTs should ensure all primary care teams have easy access to health professionals trained in examining, identifying and assessing children/young people who may be experiencing abuse or neglect, and that local arrangements include having all the necessary equipment and staff expertise for undertaking forensic medical examinations. These arrangements should avoid repeated examinations.

■ PCTs should ensure that through their contracting arrangements, independent sector providers deliver services in line with the PCT's safeguarding obligations.

Paediatricians

■ All paediatricians need to maintain their skills in recognition of abuse and be familiar with procedures to be followed if abuse/neglect is suspected.

■ When paediatricians undertake forensic medical examinations, they must ensure they are competent to do so or work with a colleague e.g. a forensic medical examiner who has the necessary complementary skills – (see 'Guidance on Paediatric Forensic Examinations in Relation to Possible Child Sexual Abuse' (2004) Royal College of Paediatrics and Child Heath and Association of Forensic Physicians at www.rcpch.ac.uk/doc.aspx?id_ Resource=1750 .

Child & Adolescent Mental Health Services (CAMHS)

- Standard 9 of the NSF is devoted to the '*Mental Health and Psychological Wellbeing of Children and Young People*'. The importance of effective partnership working is emphasized and this is especially applicable to children and young people who have mental health problems as a result of abuse and/or neglect.

- Consultation, supervision and training resources should be available and accessible in each service.

- CAMHS professionals have a role in the initial assessment process as well as in the provision of range of psychiatric and psychological assessment and treatment services for children and families e.g. court reports, direct work with children, parents and families.

Accident & Emergency (A&E) departments, ambulatory care units, walk in centres & minor injury units

- Staff working in A&E, ambulatory care units, walk in centres and minor injury units should be familiar with local procedures for making enquiries to find out whether a child is subject to a child protection plan.

- A&E staff should also be alert to the need to safeguard children's welfare when treating parents or carers of children and should be alert to carers who seek medical care from a number of sources in order to conceal the repeated nature of a child's injuries.

- The relevant child's GP should be notified of visits by children to A&E department, ambulatory care unit, walk in centre or minor injury (where the child is not registered, the appropriate contact in the PCT should be notified).

Ambulance Trusts, NHS Direct sites & walk in centres

- Staff working in Ambulance Trusts, NHS Direct sites and walk in centres have access to family homes or are involved in a time of crisis and may therefore be in a position to identify initial concerns regarding a child's welfare.

- Each of these bodies should have a named professional for child protection (see ?? for a summary of that role).

GP & other members of Primary Health Care Team (PHCT)

- The GP and other members of the Primary Health Care Team (PHCT) and practice-employed staff have key roles to play both in the identification of children who may have been, and those who have been abused as well as in subsequent intervention and protection.

■ All PHCT members should know when it is appropriate to refer a child to Children's Social Care for help as a 'child in need', and how to act on concerns that a child may be at risk of significant harm through abuse or neglect (if the GP does not make the referral, s/he should be informed at the earliest opportunity).

■ The GP, practice employed staff and the PHCT are also well placed to recognise when a parent or other adult has problems which may affect their capacity as a parent or carer, or which may mean that they pose a risk of harm to a child. The child is particularly vulnerable and the welfare of the child is paramount.

■ If the PHCT has concerns that an adul't illness or behaviour may be causing, or putting a child at risk of significant harm, staff should follow the procedures set out in chapter 5 of '*Working Together to Safeguard Children'2010* and summarised in '*What to Do If You're Worried a Child is Being Abused'.*

■ GPs, other practice staff and PHCT members have an important role with respect to information sharing (subject to normal confidentiality requirements) with Children's Social Care when enquiries are being made about a child, contributing to assessments, to involvement in a child protection plan.

■ GPS, practice staff and other PCT practitioners should make available to child protection conferences relevant information about a child and family, whether or not they – or a member of the PHCT – are able to attend.

■ PHCTs should have a clear means of identifying in records those children (together with their parents and siblings) who are the subject of a child protection plan. This will enable them to be recognised by the partners of the practice and any other doctor, practice nurse or health visitor who may be involved in the care of those children.

Maternity Services

■ The delivery of maternity services also offers an opportunity to observe attitudes towards the developing baby and to identify potential problems during pregnancy, birth and in the child's early care.

Other health professionals

■ All other health professionals and staff who provide help and support to protect children's health and development should have knowledge of LSCB procedures and how to contact named professionals for advice and support, including e.g.:

• School nurses
• Dental practitioners and dental care professionals (therapists, hygienists and nurses etc) (DCPs)

- Adult Mental Health Services (general adult and community, forensic, psychotherapy, alcohol and substance misuse and learning disability services)
- Clinical psychologists
- Staff in genito-urinary medicine services
- Obstetric and gynaecologoical staff
- Occupational therapists and physiotherapists
- Staff in sexual health services
- Speech and language therapists
- Optometrists
- Pharmacists and
- Other professional allied to medicine

Education Services

Local Authority Duty

- s.175(1) EA 2002 requires the local education authority- 'to make arrangements for ensuring that the functions conferred upon them in their capacity as a local education authority are exercised with a view to safeguarding and promoting the welfare of children'.

- *Safeguarding Children and Safer Recruitment in Education* issued in November 2006 (www.publications.teachernet.gov.uk reference number DFES 04217–2006) revised much earlier guidance and provided in a single source document advice about safeguarding, recruitment and vetting for schools and FE colleges.

- Local education authorities have the following responsibilities:

  - *Strategic*: planning, co-coordinating and liaising with other agencies and allocating resources
  - *Supportive*: ensuring maintained schools are aware of their responsibilities for child protection and monitoring their performance, making available appropriate training, model policies, advice and support and working with other agencies
  - *Operational*: taking responsibility for child protection in pupil referral units (to be re-named short term schools) and other out of school

settings, involvement in dealing with allegations against staff and volunteers, ensuring arrangements are in place to prevent unsuitable individuals from working with children

Maintained (State) Schools & Further Education (FE) Institutions

■ State schools and FE including 6th form colleges, also have a duty to exercise their functions with a view to safeguarding and promoting the welfare of pupils (aged less than 18).

■ The head teacher/principal should ensure that:

- A senior member of staff is 'designated' as taking lead responsibility for child protection, providing advice and support to staff, liaising with the authority and working with other organisations as necessary
- Staff should not themselves investigate possible abuse/neglect but play a key role by referring concerns to Children's Social Care, providing information to police investigations and/or s.47 enquiries as well as by contributing to assessments

■ Where a school age child is subject of a child protection plan, the school should be involved in its preparation and the school's role and responsibilities clearly identified.

■ Special schools, including non-maintained special schools and independent schools providing medical and/or nursing care should ensure their medical and nursing staff have appropriate training and access to advice on child protection and safeguarding and promoting children's welfare.

■ The non-statutory framework for personal, social and health education (PSHE) provides opportunities for children/young people to learn about keeping safe e.g to:

- Be taught to recognise and manage risks in different situations and then decide how to behave responsibly
- Judge what kind of physical contact is acceptable and unacceptable
- Recognise when pressure from others (including people they know) threatens personal safety and well-being and to develop effective ways of resisting pressure

■ Corporal punishment is outlawed for all pupils in all schools, including independent schools and FE institutions. The law forbids a teacher or any other member of staff using any degree of physical contact which is deliberately intended to punish a pupil or which is primarily intended to cause pain, injury or humiliation.

■ Teachers at a school are allowed to use reasonable force to control or restrain pupils under certain circumstances and other staff may do so if they have been authorised by the head teacher to have control or charge of pupils.

NB. All schools should have a policy about the use of force to control or restrain pupils and further guidance is available at www.dfes.gov.uk/ publications/guidanceonthelaw/10_98/summary. The government elected in May 2010 has announced its intention to revise the law with respect to use of physical force and searching.

Proprietors of Independent Schools

■ Independent schools, including Academies and technology colleges also have a duty to safeguard and promote the welfare of their pupils under s.157 EA 2002 and associated regulations.

■ Proprietors of independent schools should ensure that:

- Their school has a child protection policy that conforms with local guidance, is reviewed annually and is made available on request
- A senior teacher/member of staff of the senior management team is designated to take responsibility for dealing with child protection issues
- The proprietor, head teacher and designated teacher have attended the necessary training to equip them to carry out their responsibilities for child protection which is kept up to date and high quality training is available for all other staff appropriate to their needs
- Any deficiencies or weaknesses are remedied without delay

- They have arrangements in place to liaise and work with other agencies over child protection issues in line with policies and procedures
- They have safe recruitment procedures in place together with procedures for dealing with allegations of abuse against staff

NB. Boarding schools, residential special schools and FE institutions that provide accommodation for under 18s must have regard to the respective National Standards which may be found at www.csci.org.uk/ inforamtionforserviceproviders/ nationalminimumstandards

Schools Governors & Governing Bodies

- S.175(2) EA 2002 states that the governing body of a maintained school shall make arrangements for ensuring their functions relating to conduct of the school are exercised with a view to safeguarding and promoting the welfare of pupils at the school.

- S.175(3) states the governing body of an institution within the further education sector must make arrangements for ensuring that their functions relating to the conduct of the institution are exercised with a view to safeguarding and promoting the welfare of children receiving education or training at the institution.

- Guidance states that governing bodies and FE corporations should ensure that:

- School or institution has a child protection policy that is reviewed annually, referred to in the school/institution's prospectus, and that conforms to LEA and LSCB policy and guidance
- Policy includes provision for procedures for recruiting and selecting staff and volunteers and for dealing with allegations of abuse against staff and volunteers
- School/institution has a senior teacher/member of senior management team designated to take lead responsibility for dealing with child protection issues
- Members of the governing body/corporation, head teacher , designated teacher/person and all other staff and volunteers who work with children have attended appropriate training to equip them to carry out their responsibilities for child protection effectively and that this is kept up to date
- Any deficiencies or weaknesses in regard to child protection arrangements are brought to the attention of the governing body/corporation and remedied without delay
- A member of the governing body/corporation is nominated to be responsible for liaising with the LEA and/or partner agencies, as appropriate in the event of allegations of abuse being made against the head teacher or principal

NB. S.175 (4) EA 2002 states that 'an authority or body mentioned in any of subsections 1–3 shall, in considering what arrangements are required to be made by them under that subsection, have regard to any guidance given from time to time in relation to England by the Secretary of State or in relation to Wales by the National Assembly for Wales.

S.175 (5) states that in this section 'child means a person under the age of 18; governing body in relation to an institution within the further education sector has the meaning given by s.90 Further and Higher Education Act 1992; maintained school means a community foundation or voluntary school, a community or foundation special school or a maintained nursery school.

Education Welfare Officers

- In their direct welfare work with families, EWOs may recognise child protection issues and must refer these to Children's Social Care.

- EWOs should assist the designated teacher in monitoring children for whom a child protection plan is in place.

- EWOs are able to provide advice and support to other education staff on child protection matters.

OfSTED

- OfSTED will inspect the extent to which LEAs, schools and FE institutions discharge their duties under s.175 EA 2002.

Other Agencies & Wider Community

■ The following agencies also have a direct contribution (detailed in *Working Together to Safeguard Children* 2010) with respect to prevention or reporting, as well as a supportive role in investigation of, abuse and neglect:

- Housing authorities and registered social landlords (RSLs)
- Children and Family Courts Advisory and Support Service (CAFCASS) [in Wales CAFCASS Cymru] (duty under s.12(1) CJCA 2000 to safeguard and protect the welfare of children involved in family proceedings in which their welfare is, or may be in question)
- Sports, cultural and leisure services inc. libraries, museums and art centres
- Youth and community workers (YCWs)
- Youth offending teams (YOTs)
- National Offender Management Service (Probation and Prisons)
- Young offender institutions (YOIs), secure training centres (STCs) and local authority secure children's homes (LASCHs)
- Childcare services (family and children's centres, day nurseries, childminders, pre-schools, playgroups and holiday and out of school schemes)
- Armed services
- Faith groups/churches

- Fire & Rescue services
- Connexions (currently providing services under s.114 Learning and Skills Act 2000)
- Ofsted
- Immigration & Nationality Department (IND)
- All other organisations which deal with children

■ The support of the wider community should also be encouraged by means of:

- Open communication with local people and media about agencies' work
- Provision of accessible information and advice in a form which is clear and relevant to all
- Publicising and promoting how and when to make contact where concerns about a child exist and what response to expect
- Offering advice and training to community, religious and other voluntary groups on how to provide a safe service to children

Local Safeguarding Children Boards (LSCB)

Duty to Establish & Composition of LSCBs

■ Each CSA in England must establish a LSCB for its area and the Board must include representative/s of the authority by which it is established and each 'Board partner' as prescribed in the LSCB Regulations 2006 (SI 2006/90).

NB. The material below reflects the amendments introduced by the Local Safeguarding Children Board (Amendment) Regulations 2010 SI 2010/622 introduced by s.13(4) Children Act 2004.

■ Each of the following is a 'Board partner' set out in s.13(3) Children Act 2004:

- Where the authority is a county council for an area for which there is also a district council, the district council
- The chief officer of Police for a Police area any part of which falls within the area of the authority
- The Local Probation Trust for an area any part of which falls within the area of the authority
- The YOT for an area any part of which falls within the area of the authority
- The Strategic Health Authority (SHA) and a Primary Care Trust (PCT) for an area any part of which falls within the area of the authority

- An NHS Trust and an NHS foundation Trust all or most of whose hospitals, establishments and facilities are situated in the area of the authority
- A person providing services under s.114 Learning and Skills Act 2000 in any part of the area of the authority (currently Connexions)
- CAFCASS
- The governor of any secure training centre (STC) in the area of the authority (or, in the case of a contracted out STC, its director)
- The governor of any prison in the area of the authority which ordinarily detains children (or, in the case of a contracted out prison, its director)

NB. 2 or more Board partners may be represented by the same person and the CSA or any other partner may have 2 or more representatives and an LSCB may cover more than a single area.

■ S.196(1) Apprenticeships, Skills, Children and Learning Act 2009 amends s.13 and s.14 Children Act 2004 and provides for the appointment of 2 local community representatives to each LSCB in England.

■ With effect from 01.04.10 local authorities have had to take all reasonable steps to ensure that schools are represented on the LSCB i.e. by a governing body of a maintained school, proprietor of a non-maintained special school, proprietor of a city technology college, a city college for the technology of the arts or an Academy and the governing body of a further education institution, the main site of which is situated in the authority's area.

■ The local authority should also secure the involvement of the NSPCC and other relevant national and local organisations. At a minimum, local organisations should include faith groups, children's centres, GPs, independent healthcare organisations and voluntary and community sector organisations including those providing specialist care to children with severe disabilities and complex health needs.

■ In area where they have significant local activity, the LSCB *may* also include representatives of the Armed Forces or the UKBA.

■ *Working Together to Safeguard Children* 2010 (para.3.83) also lists a large number of other agencies and groups e.g. domestic violence forums that the LSCB may need to make appropriate arrangements to engage in its work as needed.

LSCB Relationship with Wider Arrangements to Improve Outcomes for Children

■ The work of LSCBs is part of the wider context of Children's Trust arrangements that aim to achieve the 5 'Every Child Matters Outcomes' for all children. The particular focus of LSCBs is on the 'staying safe' outcome

Chairing of LSCB

■ It is the responsibility of the authority which establishes an LSCB, after consultation with Board partners, to appoint a chair. There should be a presumption that the chair will be someone independent of the local agencies so that the LSCB can exercise its local challenge function effectively. *Working Together* 2010 acknowledges that it may take some time to develop sufficient availability of suitable independent chairs and indicates that it is expected that LSCBs will work toward this over time.

Objectives & Scope of LSCBs

■ The overall objectives of LSCBs (set out in s.14(1) Children Act 2004) are to:

• Co-ordinate what is done by each person or body represented on the Board for the purposes of safeguarding and promoting the welfare of children in the area
• Ensure the effectiveness of what is done by each such person or body for that purpose

■ The scope of LSCB's role may be conveniently divided into the 3 areas summarised below.

■ *Preventive work* affects all children and aims to prevent maltreatment, or impairment of health or development, and ensure children are growing up in circumstances consistent with the provision of safe and effective care, and can include:

- Mechanisms to identify abuse and neglect wherever they occur
- Work to increase understanding of safeguarding children issues in the professional and wider communities, promoting the message that safeguarding is everybody's responsibility
- Work to ensure that organisations working or in contact with children operate recruitment and human resources practices that take account of the need to safeguard and promote children's welfare
- Monitoring the effectiveness of organisations' implementation of their duties under s.11 Children Act 2004
- Ensuring children know who they can contact when they have concerns about their own or others' safety and welfare
- Ensuring that adults (including those who are harming children) know who they can contact if they have a concern about a child/young person
- Work to prevent accidents and other injuries and when possible, deaths
- Work to prevent and respond effectively to bullying

■ *Proactive work* aims to target particular groups, e.g.:

- Developing and evaluating thresholds and procedures for work with families whose child has been identified as 'in need', but when the child is not suffering or at risk of suffering significant harm

- Work to safeguard and promote the welfare of groups of children who are potentially more vulnerable than the general population, e.g. children who have run away from home, are missing from school or childcare, those in the youth justice system inc. custody, disabled children and those affected by gangs

■ *Responsive/individual work* protects children who are suffering, or are at risk of suffering harm including:

- Children abused and neglected within families, including those harmed in the context of domestic violence or as a consequence of the impact of substance misuse or parental mental ill health
- Children abused outside families by adults known to them
- Children abused and neglected by professional carers, within an institutional settings, or anywhere else where children are cared for away from home
- Children abused by strangers
- Children abused by other young people
- Young perpetrators of abuse
- Children abused through sexual exploitation and
- Young victims of crime

Functions of LSCBs

■ In order to achieve the objectives defined by s.14 (1) Children Act 2004, the LSCB has the following functions defined in reg.5 of the LSCB Regulations 2006 (SI No. 90).

■ The LSCB must develop *policies and procedures* for safeguarding and promoting the welfare of children in the area, inc. those in relation to:

- Action to be taken where there are concerns about a child's safety or welfare, including thresholds for intervention
- Training of persons who work with children or in services affecting the safety and welfare of children

NB. Though some may decide to organise and deliver training, this is not part of the core requirements for LSCBs.

- Recruitment and supervision of persons who work with children
- Investigation of allegations concerning persons working with children
- Safety and welfare of children who are privately fostered
- Co-operation with neighbouring authorities and their Board partners

■ The LSCB should:

- Communicate to persons and bodies in its area the need to safeguard and promote the welfare of children, *raising awareness* of how this can best be done and encouraging them to do so

- *Monitor and evaluate effectiveness* of what is done by the authority and its Board partners individually and collectively to safeguard and promote the welfare of children, and advise them on ways to improve
- *Produce and publish an annual report* on the effectiveness of safeguarding in the local area (and copied to the Children's Trust Board)
- *Participate in planning and commissioning* of local services for children
- *Collect and analyse information about all child deaths*
- *Undertake serious case reviews (SCRs)* (see p.63) advising the authority and its Board partners on lessons to be learned

■ Para. 3.26 of *Working Together to Safeguard Children* 2010 lists a number of additional subjects that may require local protocols or multi agency procedures:

- Simple means of resolving professional differences of view in a specific case e.g. should a child protection conference be convened
- Attendance at child protection conferences including quora
- Attendance at family group conferences
- Involving children and family members in conferences, role of advocates, criteria for excluding parents in exceptional circumstances

- A decision making process for the need for a child protection plan based upon the view of the agencies present at the conference
- Handling complaints from families about the functioning of child protection conferences
- A procedure for handling complaints regarding requests to share information

■ An LSCB may also engage in any other activity that facilitates, or is conducive to, the achievement of its main objectives

■ LSCBs are not front-line delivery organisations. Their objectives are to co-ordinate and ensure the effectiveness of what member organisations do, and to contribute to broader delivery/commissioning arrangements through the Children and Young People's Plan (CYPP).

Monitoring & Inspection Role

■ *Working Together to Safeguard Children* 2010 indicates LSCBs should ensure the effectiveness of safeguarding work of member organisations by means of a peer review process based on:

- Self evaluation
- Performance indicators and
- Joint audit

■ Where it is found that a Board partner is not performing effectively in safeguarding and promoting the welfare of children, and the LSCB is not convinced that any planned action to improve performance will be adequate, the LSCB chair or a member or employee designated by the chair should explain these concerns to those individuals and organisations that need be aware of the failing and may be able to take action, e.g. to the most senior individual/s in the organisation, to the relevant monitoring bodies and, if necessary, to the relevant government department.

LSCB Links with the Children's Trust Board

- The responsibilities of the LSCB are complementary to those of the Children's Trust; its particular role is to ensure the effectiveness of the arrangements made by wider partnership and individual agencies to safeguard and promote the welfare of children

- An LSCB is not an operational sub-committee of the Children's Trust Board and should not be subordinate to nor subsumed within the Children's Trust Board structures in a way that might compromise its separate identity and independent voice.

- There should be agreed local protocols between the LSCB and the Children's Trust Board to ensure that the LSCB is able to challenge and scrutinise effectively the work of the Children's Trust Board and partners.

- The LSCB must be able to form a view of the quality of local activity, to challenge organisations as necessary and to speak with an independent voice.

Thus, the LSCB and Children's Trust Board should be chaired by different people.

■ The Children's Trust Board should work with the LSCB to agree:

- A strategic approach to understanding needs, including a sophisticated analysis of data and effective engagement with children, young people and families
- A clear approach to understanding the effectiveness of current services, and identifying priorities for change – including when services need to be reshaped to developed
- Integrated and effective arrangements for ensuring that priorities for change are delivered in practice through the Children and Young People's Plan
- Effective approaches to understand the impact of specialist services on outcomes for children, young people and families and using this understanding constructively to challenge lack of progress and drive further improvement

Serious Case Reviews (SCRs)

■ Regulation 5(1) (e) of the LSCB Regulation 2006 requires LSCBs to instigate a serious case review (SCR) in specified circumstances and *Working Together to Safeguard Children* 2010 defines in chapter 8 of that guidance, those circumstances in which an SCR should be initiated and how it is to be conducted.

- The purpose of a SCR is to:

  - Establish what lessons are to be learned from the case about the way in which local professionals and organisations work individually and together to safeguard children
  - Identify clearly what those lessons are both within and between agencies, how and within hat timescales they will be acted upon and what is expected to change as a result, and hence
  - Improve intra and inter-agency working and better safeguard and promote the welfare of children

  NB. SCRs are not inquiries into how a child died or who is culpable which matters are for Coroners and criminal courts respectively.

- A LSCB should *always* undertake a SCR when a child dies (including death by suspected suicide) *and* abuse or neglect is known or suspected to be factor in the death (irrespective of whether Children's Social Care was involved with the family).

- These SCRs should include situations when a child has been killed by a parent, carer or close relative with a mental illness, known to misuse substances or to perpetrate domestic abuse. In addition a SCR should always be carried out if a child dies in custody (Police custody, on remand or following sentencing, in a Young Offender Institution or Secure Training Centre or secure children's home) or if the child was detained under then Mental Health Act 2005.

■ The LSCB should always consider the justification for a SCR when:

- A child sustains a potentially life-threatening injury or serious and permanent impairment of health or development through abuse or neglect
- A child has been seriously harmed as a result of being subjected to sexual abuse or
- A parent has been murdered and a domestic homicide review is being initiated under the Domestic Violence Act 2004 or
- A child has been seriously harmed following a violent assault perpetrated by another child or adult *and*
- The case gives rise to concerns about inter-agency working to protect children

NB. Para. 8.12 of Working Together to Safeguard Children 2010 offers further guidance on determining whether a SCR might be useful in specific circumstances.

Child Death Reviews

■ Reg. 6 LSCB Regulations 2006 requires that each LSCB (in England) in relation to the deaths of children ordinarily resident in its area:

- Collect and analyse information about each death with a view to identifying any case giving rise to the need for a SCR; any matters of concern affecting the safety and welfare of children in its area and any wider public health or safety concerns arising from a particular death or a pattern of deaths in the area

- Put in place procedures for ensuring that there is a co-ordinated response by the authority, its Board partners and other relevant persons, to an 'unexpected death'

■ There are two interrelated processes for reviewing child deaths (either of which can trigger a SCR):

- The *rapid response* by a group of key professionals who come together for the purpose of enquiring into and evaluating each unexpected death of a child
- An overview of all child deaths up to the age of 18 (excluding stillborn babies and planned lawful terminations in the LSCB area, undertaken by a child death overview panel (CDOP)

■ Chapter 7 of *Working Together to Safeguard Children* 2010 provides additional guidance.

Notes

LAW

Primary Legislation

■ The main sources of English primary legislation relating to the safeguarding and protection of children are:

- Children Act 1989
- Provisions of Criminal Justice Act 1991 (as amended) relating to use of video recording in criminal proceedings
- Part IV Family Law Act 1996
- Protection of Children Act 1999
- Protection From Harassment Act 1997
- Education Act 2002
- Sexual Offences Act 2003
- Children Act 2004
- Safeguarding Vulnerable Groups Act 2006
- Children and Young Persons Act 2008

■ In discharging any of their responsibilities, including child protection s.6 HRA 1998 requires all 'public authorities' e.g. Children's Social Care, Health Trusts, Police, courts etc, to act toward children and adults in ways which are compatible with the European Convention on Human Rights with respect to:

- Article 2 Respect to Life
- Article 3 Prohibition of Torture
- Article 4 Prohibition of Slavery and Forced Labour
- Article 5 Right to Liberty and Security
- Article 6 Right to a Fair Trial

- Article 7 No Punishment Without Law
- Article 8 Right to Respect for Private and Family Life
- Article 9 Freedom of Thought, Conscience and Religion
- Article 10 Freedom of Expression
- Article 11 Freedom of Assembly and Association
- Article 12 Right to Marry

■ Article 14 of the Convention provides that the enjoyment of the above rights must be allowed without discrimination on any ground such as sex, race, colour, language, religion, political or other opinion, national or social origin, association with a national minority, property, birth or other status.

■ A key concept of the Convention of particular relevance to child protection work is that of 'proportionality' i.e. any interference with a person's rights must be sanctioned by law, go no further than necessary and be proportionate to meet a 'pressing social need'.

■ For example, with respect to Article 8 – Respect for Private and Family Life, public authorities can override the right if it is necessary for 'public safety, to prevent crime, to protect health or morals or for the protection of the rights and freedoms of others'.

Inter Agency Co-operation [s.27 CA 1989]

- There is a mutual obligation on local authorities to assist one another unless this is in conflict with their own statutory duties.

Co-operation to Improve Well Being [s.10 CA 2004 England; s.25 Wales]

- Each CSA must make arrangements to promote co-operation between:

  - The authority
  - Each of the authority's relevant partners and
  - Such other persons or bodies as it considers appropriate engaged in activities in relation to children in the authority's area

- Arrangements are to be made with a view to improving well-being of children in the area so far as relating to:

  - Physical and mental health
  - Protection from harm and neglect
  - Education, training and recreation
  - The contribution made by them to society
  - Emotional, social and economic well-being

- The relevant partners of a CSA in must co-operate with the authority in the making of such arrangements.

**Arrangements to Safeguard & Promote Welfare
[s.11 CA 2004 England; s.28 Wales]**

- S.11 (England) and s.28 (Wales) apply to each of the
  following:

  - A Children's Services Authority
  - A district council which is not such an authority
    [England only]
  - A Local Health Board [Wales only]
  - A Strategic Health Authority [England only]
  - A Special Health Authority, so far as exercising
    functions in relation to England, designated by
    order by the Secretary of State for the purpose of
    s.11 [England only]
  - A PCT or NHS Trust all or most of whose
    hospitals, establishments and facilities are
    situated in England [England only]
  - An NHS Trust all or most of whose hospitals,
    establishments and facilities are situated in
    Wales [Wales only]
  - An NHS Foundation Trust [England only]
  - The Police Authority and its chief officer
  - The British Transport Police Authority
  - A local Probation Board for an area
  - A YOT for an area
  - The governor of a prison or secure training centre
    (or, in the case of a contracted out prison or
    secure training centre, its director)
  - Any person to the extent that s/he is providing
    services in pursuance of s.74 Education and Skills

Act 2008 (in England) and s.123(1)(b) (Youth Services in Wales) Learning and Skills Act 2000

■ Each of the above person and bodies must make arrangements for ensuring that:

• Their functions are discharged having regard to the need to safeguard and promote the welfare of children and
• Any services provided by another person pursuant to arrangements made by the person or body in the discharge of their functions are provided having regard to that need

■ s.175(1) EA 2002 requires the LEA 'to make arrangements for ensuring that the functions conferred upon them in their capacity as a local education authority are exercised with a view to safeguarding and promoting the welfare of children' (see p.44)

Prevention of Neglect and Abuse [Sch.2 Para. 4 CA 1989]

■ Each local authority must take reasonable steps through provision of family support services to prevent children within its area suffering ill treatment or neglect.

■ The local authority must inform any other local authority if a child likely to suffer harm lives, or proposes to live in its area.

Local Authority Duty to Make Enquiries [s.47(1) (a) (i) – (iii) (b) CA 1989 as amended by CDA 1998]

■ When told a child is subject of an Emergency Protection Order, Police Powers of Protection (see below), or the local authority has reasonable cause to *suspect* s/he is suffering/likely to suffer 'significant harm', or has contravened a ban imposed under the Crime and Disorder Act 1998, it must make enquiries to enable a decision on any necessary action to safeguard and promote the child's welfare.

NB. The fact it need only be reasonable cause to suspect rather than believe was emphasised in R (On the Application of S) v Swindon BC & Another [2001] 3 FCR 702. Curfew contravention enquiries must be begun as soon as practicable and in any case within 48 hours of receiving information [s.47 (1)(a)(iii) CA 1989 inserted by s.15(4) CDA 1998].

■ It is the duty of any local authority, education, housing or health trust, and the NSPCC (unless unreasonable to do so) to assist these enquiries e.g. provision of relevant information and advice [s.47 (9); (11) CA 1989].

NB. S.53 CA 2004 amended s.47 CA 1989 so that there now exists an obligation on the local authority to seek the wishes and feelings of the child and (having regard to age and understanding) give them due consideration when undertaking enquiries.

■ In Z v the UK [2001] 2 FLR 612(Formerly X v Bedfordshire CC) (HL), the European Court, ruled that failure by Bedfordshire County Council over 4 years to respond appropriately to concerns about 4 children who were victims of abuse and neglect by their parents, disclosed a breach of their human rights under Articles 3 (Freedom From Degrading Or Inhuman Treatment), and Article 13 (No Access To An Effective Remedy).

Provision of Accommodation to Protect Child [Sch.2 Para.5 CA 1989]

■ If it appears to a local authority that a child living on particular premises is suffering or is likely to suffer ill treatment at the hands of another person living there, and that other person proposes to move out, the local authority may assist her/him to obtain alternative accommodation.

Emergency Protection Order (EPO) [s.44 CA 1989]

Applications

■ By anyone without notice to the other parties, to a court or an individual magistrate.

NB. It has been argued in Scotland that such applications being made without notice are in breach of Article 6 (Right To a Fair Trial). Reference might also be made the 'proportionality principle' [see above].

Grounds

■ A court must be satisfied that:

- There is reasonable cause to believe child is likely to suffer 'significant harm' if not removed to accommodation provided by the applicant or does not remain in current location e.g. hospital [s.44 (1) (a) CA 1989] or
- The local authority or NSPCC enquiry is at risk of being frustrated by unreasonable refusal of access [s.44 (1) (b) or (c) respectively].

NB. The social worker or NSPCC officer must produce identification. Early morning removal of a child is only justified if clear grounds exist that significant harm would otherwise occur or where vital evidence is obtainable only by such means [Re A (Minors) [1992] 1 All ER 153] and is proportionate to the end sought to be achieved (i.e. protection of the health of children – Articles 8(1) & (2) of the Convention). For

*the meaning of 'reasonable cause to suspect' here
and in s. 47, see R on the app of S v Swindon
Borough Council [2001] 3 FCR 702.*

Effect

- Gives applicant parental responsibility and right to
  remove/prevent removal of child.

- If, during the course of an EPO, it appears to the
  applicant that it would be safe to return the child/
  allow her/him to leave the place in which s/he has
  been detained, the applicant must do this.

- If the child is returned home and it proves necessary
  (within the time limit of the EPO) the order can be
  reactivated.

Duration [s.45]

- Up to 8 days with 1 possible extension up to a
  further 7 days.

- If the last day of an 8 day order falls on a public
  holiday (Christmas, Good Friday, a Bank Holiday or
  Sunday) the court may specify a period which ends at
  noon on the first later day which is not a public
  holiday.

Exclusion Requirements in Emergency Protection Orders [s.44A CA 1989 as inserted by s.52 & Sch.6 FLA 1996]

- Provisions described below enable the court when making an EPO to attach an exclusion requirement so a suspected abuser can be removed/kept away from the home in which child is living, or the surrounding area.

  NB. 'Without notice' orders may offend against Article 6 and especially in attaching exclusion requirements where it may also be argued there is a potential breach of Article 1 Protocol 1 of the Convention (Right to Peaceful Enjoyment of Possessions),i.e. one's home.

- When the court is satisfied that the threshold criteria for an EPO are satisfied and it makes such an order, the court may also include an exclusion requirement *if* the following conditions are satisfied:

  - There is reasonable cause to believe if the 'relevant person' is excluded from a dwelling-house in which the child lives, the child will not be likely to suffer significant harm either if s/he is not removed (ie. s.44(1)(a)(i)), or does not remain (ie. s.44(1)(a)(ii), or because enquiries as per s.44(1) (b) or (c) will cease to be frustrated

  - Another person living in same dwelling-house (parent or not) is able and willing to give to the child the care which it would be reasonable to

give her/him and that person consents to the inclusion of the exclusion requirement.

NB. An argument could be made in respect of potential breaches of Article 8 and Article 1 Protocol 1 of the Convention, and the proportionality principle previously referred to is also relevant.

- An 'exclusion requirement' for the purposes of s.44A CA 1989 is any one or more of the following provisions:

  - Requiring the relevant person to leave a dwelling-house in which s/he is living with a child
  - Prohibiting the relevant person from entering a dwelling-house in which the child lives
  - Excluding the relevant person from a defined area in which a dwelling-house in which the child lives is situated [s.44A(5) CA 1989 as inserted by s.52 & Sch.6 FLA 1996]

Duration of Exclusion Requirement in Emergency Protection Order [s.44A (4) CA 1989 as inserted by s.52 & Sch. 6 FLA 1996]

- The court may provide that the exclusion requirement is to have effect for a shorter period than the other provisions of the order.

  NB. There is no power to extend exclusion requirements beyond interim or EPO stage and if continuing protection is sought, an application must be made by person with whom the child living, for an

injunction under s.100 or perhaps a Prohibited Steps Order.

Power of Arrest [s.44A (5) CA 1989 as inserted by s.52 & Sch.6 FLA 1996]

- The exclusion requirement may have a power of arrest attached to it [s.44A (5)].Where it does so, the court may provide that the power of arrest is to have effect for a shorter period than the exclusion requirement [s.44A (6) CA 1989 as inserted by s.52 & Sch.6 FLA 1996].

  NB. Any period specified for the purposes of ss. (4) or (6) may be extended by the court on one or more occasions on an application to vary or discharge the EPO [s.44A (7) CA 1989 as inserted by s.52 & Sch.7 FLA 1996].

- When a power of arrest is attached to an exclusion requirement of an EPO, a constable may arrest without warrant any person whom s/he has reasonable grounds to believe to be in breach of the requirement [s.44A(8) CA 1989 as inserted by s.52 & Sch.6 FLA 1996].

- If while an EPO containing an exclusion requirement is in force, the applicant has removed the child from the dwelling-house from which the relevant person is excluded, to other accommodation for a continuous period of over 24 hours, the order shall cease to have effect in so far as it imposes the exclusion

requirement [s.44A (10) CA 1989 as inserted by s.52 & Sch.6 FLA 1996].

Undertakings Relating To Emergency Protection Orders [s.44B CA 1989 as inserted by s.52 & Sch.6 FLA 1996]

- ■ In any case where the court has power to include an exclusion requirement in an EPO, the court may accept an undertaking from the relevant person and in such cases no power of arrest may be attached [s.44B(1) & (2) CA 1989 as inserted by s.52 & Sch.6 FLA 1996].

- ■ Such an undertaking:

  - • Is enforceable as if it were an order of the court
  - • Will cease to have effect if, whilst it is in force, the applicant has removed the child from the dwelling-house from which relevant person is excluded to other accommodation for a continuous period of more than 24 hours [s.44B(3) CA 1989 as inserted by s.52 & Sch.6 FLA 1996]

- ■ On the application of a person who is not entitled to apply for the order to be discharged, but is a person to whom an exclusion requirement contained in the order applies, an EPO may be varied or discharged by the court in so far as it imposes the exclusion requirement [s.45(8A) CA 1989 as inserted by s.52 & Sch.6 FLA 1996].

- When a power of arrest has been attached to an exclusion requirement of EPO the court may, on the application of any person entitled to apply for the discharge of the order so far as it imposes the exclusion requirement, vary or discharge the order in so far as it confers a power of arrest (regardless of whether any application has been made to vary or discharge any other provision of the order) [s.45 (8B) CA 1989 as inserted by s.52 & Sch.6 FLA 1996].

Challenge of EPO

- An application for a discharge can be made by parent, person with parental responsibility, child or anyone with whom child living at time of EPO.

- So as to ensure compatibility with the European Convention on Human Rights, s.30 C&YPA 2008 revoked the previous 72 restriction on applying for a discharge of an EPO.

  NB. Reasonable contact is assumed between child and above parties and can only be restricted by court direction. A court may be asked for/may give directions to limit contact and/or about medical/psychiatric examinations. A child of 'sufficient understanding' or aged 16 or over may refuse examination.

Discovery [s.48 (1) CA 1989]

- If necessary, a court may direct someone to disclose to applicant for EPO the whereabouts of a child.

NB. A statement or admission made in complying with a court direction to disclose a child's whereabouts is not admissible in evidence against person or spouse in proceedings other than perjury.

Entry/ Search [s.48 (3) CA 1989]

■ An EPO may include directions to enter and search (but not by force).

Warrant [s.48 (9) and (10) CA 1989]

■ Where a court believes applicant has been/is likely to be refused access to child it may issue a warrant to police to assist, using if necessary, reasonable force.

NB. The court can direct that police be accompanied by a doctor, nurse or health visitor.

Police Powers of Protection (P.P.O.P) [s46 CA 1989]

Grounds [s.46 (1) CA 1989]

■ Police must have reasonable grounds to believe child would otherwise suffer 'significant harm'.

NB. P.P.O.P. may arguably breach Article 8(1)(Right To Respect for Private and Family Life). Although Article 8(2) qualifies this right, the public authority's interference must be 'proportionate'.

Effect

■ A P.P.O.P.:

- Allows a police constable to remove and accommodate child, or
- Ensure that s/he remains in current location
- Does not give parental responsibility
- Does allow police to do all that is reasonable

Duration [s.46 (6) CA 1989]

■ Up to 72 hours.

Conditions

■ Police must:

- Inform parent, local authority and child of steps taken [s.46 (3) and (4)], and

- Transfer her/him as soon as possible to local authority accommodation, though the responsibility for ongoing enquiries and any decision to release child from police protection remains with the Police.

NB. Police can also apply for an EPO to be made in favour of a local authority. If so, any time spent in police protection must be deducted from time on EPO.

Current Home Office guidance may be found in HO 17/2008 which re-states and clarifies duties and powers of the Police under s.46 CA 1989.

Recovery Order [s.50 CA 1989]

Applications

- Local authority, N.S.P.C.C. and Police if child on EPO or C.O. (including interim C.O.).

- Police if subject of P.P.O.P.

Grounds

- Child is subject to Care Order, EPO or in Police protection, has run away or is being kept away from a responsible person who should be caring for her/ him, or is missing

Effect

- Directs responsible person to produce child or to inform of whereabouts.

- Authorises Police to search (using reasonable force if necessary), and

- Allows removal of child by authorised person.

- If foster carers, private or voluntary homes have a certificate from the Secretary of State, they are exempt from law covering abduction of children.

Child Assessment Order (C.A.O.) [s.43 CA 1989]

Applications

■ By local authority or N.S.P.C.C. [s.43 (1) CA 1989].

NB. Applicant must provide 7 days notice to persons listed in s.43 (11) and a court can treat the application as if it were for an EPO [s.43 (3) CA 1989].

Grounds [s.43 (1) CA 1989]

■ Applicant must satisfy the court that s/he has reasonable cause to suspect child is suffering or is likely to suffer 'significant harm', and

- Needs an assessment of the state of the child's health or development or way in which s/he has been treated to determine if s/he is suffering or likely to suffer 'significant harm', and that the
- Assessment is otherwise unlikely to be undertaken or to be satisfactory

NB. For a case where a local authority was reluctant to pay for a court ordered assessment but the House of Lords ordered it to proceed see Re C (Interim Care Order: Residential Assessment) [1997] 1 FLR 1.

Effect [s.43 (6) CA 1989]

■ Obliges person/s to produce child and comply with court directions e.g. medicals and any other form of assessment – see Re C [1997] 1 FLR 1 [HL].

NB. If of sufficient understanding or aged 16 or over, a child may refuse medical. If necessary, child may be kept from home.

Duration [s.43 (6) CA 1989]

■ From a specified date and for such period, not exceeding 7 days, which may be specified.

Rights of Refusal of Medical & Other Assessment [ss.38; 43; 44 CA 1989]

■ The right of a child to refuse to submit to medical, psychiatric or dental investigations is limited to the assessment stages of the order provided for the above sections.

NB. For the circumstances in which the child's refusal may be overruled, see South Glamorgan CC v W and B [1993] 1 FLR 574 where the High Court's inherent jurisdiction under s.100 CA 1989 was invoked to override the refusal of a 15 year old to psychiatric assessment in an interim Care Order s.38(6) direction.

Risk Reduction

- *Chapter 12 of Working Together to Safeguard Children* 2010 provides practice guidance and information about a range of mechanisms when managing adults, or children and young people identified as presenting a risk or potential risk of harm to children.

- Guidance on offences against children (Home Office Circular 16/2005) at www.homeoffice.gov.uk/about-us/publications/home-office-circulars/circulars-2005/016–2005/index.html explains how those people who present a risk or potential risk to children should be identified.

- *Multi Agency Public Protection Arrangements* (MAPPA) provides a national framework in England and Wales for assessment and management of risk of serious harm by specified sexual and violent offenders (inc. young people).

- *National MAPPA guidance (2009) at www.probation.homeoffice.gov.uk/output/page30.asp* further develops processes particularly with regard to young people who pose a risk and the role of YOTs.

- *Visor* is a national database which currently carries details of MAPPA eligible offenders and other potentially dangerous individuals. Police, Probation and Prison Service have access to it.

■ *The National Offender Management System* (NOMS) assesses risk of serious harm using the Offender Assessment System (OASys) supplemented by additional assessment procedures. The Youth justice Board uses ASSET for under 18 year olds.

■ *Multi-agency Risk Assessment Conferences (MARACs)* are meetings which have the safety of high risk victims of domestic abuse as their focus.

■ The MARAC is a process involving the participation of all key statutory and voluntary agencies which might be involved in supporting a victim of domestic abuse.

■ *The Vetting and Barring Scheme* that aims to ensure that unsuitable people do not work with children on a paid or voluntary basis comprises:

  • Two barred lists maintained by the Independent Safeguarding Authority (ISA), one for children and one for vulnerable adults
  • A register of those wishing to work with vulnerable groups

NB. The government is proposing changes to the previous implementation plan for the vetting and barring scheme. Latest guidance should be sought from the ISA website at www.isa-gov.org.uk

KEY FACTORS SUPPORTING EFFECTIVE CHILD PROTECTION

Clarity

■ Achieving good outcomes for children is dependent upon working together to an agreed plan and effective inter agency collaboration requires organisations and people to be clear about:

- Their roles and responsibilities
- The purpose of their activities, decisions required at each stage of the process and the planned outcomes for child/family
- The legislative basis for the work
- Policies and procedures to be followed including the way in which information will be shared within and across professions and how this will be recorded
- Which organisation, team or professional has lead responsibility, the precise roles of others who are involved including child/family
- Any timescales in regulations or guidance which govern completion of assessments, formulation of plans and their review

■ Research suggests that work to safeguard and promote children's welfare should, in principle:

- Be child centred
- Be rooted in child development
- Be focused on outcomes for children
- Be holistic in approach
- Ensure equality of opportunity
- Involve children and families

- Build on strengths as well as identifying difficulties
- Be integrated in approach
- Represent a continuing process not an event
- Be about provision of services to meet immediate and longer term need and be regularly reviewed
- Be informed by evidence

Sensitivity to Race, Racism & Cultural Needs

- Children from black and minority ethnic groups and their parents are likely to have experienced harassment, and discrimination and such experiences are likely to affect their responses to assessment and enquiry processes.

- So as to make sensitive and informed professional judgements about a child's needs, professionals must also be sensitive to differing family patterns, lifestyles and child rearing patterns which vary across racial, ethnic and cultural groups.

- The need for neutral, high quality, gender-appropriate translation or interpreting services should be taken into account when working with children and families whose preferred language is not English.

- Professionals must guard against positive or negative myths and stereotypes about black and other minority ethnic families.

- The focus of work must remain always on the needs of individual children.

- It is critical that families understand the child protection process and professionals should provide clear, accessible oral and written information (where necessary, in the family's preferred language).

Information Sharing & Confidentiality

- Research and experience indicates that to keep children safe professionals must share relevant information across geographical and professional boundaries.

- Information relevant to child protection will be about:

  - Health and development of a child and her/his exposure to possible harm
  - A parent/carer who is unable to care adequately for a child
  - Other individuals who may present a risk of harm to the child

- The duty of all professionals providing services to adults or to children is to place the needs of the child first.

- Doctors, nurses and other health staff, teachers and social workers should be confident that their practice with respect to information sharing is both lawful and in accordance with required professional standards.

- Each case will depend upon its own facts. Legal advice should be sought from agencies' advisers if a professional is concerned about the legality of sharing information.

Relevant Law & Official Guidance

■ The main sources of relevant law and official guidance about information sharing and confidentiality are:

- Common law
- European Convention on Human Rights
- Data Protection Act 1998
- The Caldicott Standards (which apply to health and social services)
- Children Act 1989
- Cross government 'Information Sharing: Guidance for practitioners and managers' at www.dcsf.gov.uk/ecm/informationsharing

■ The '*Common Law Duty of Confidence*' requires that personal information about children and families kept by professionals and agencies should not generally be disclosed without the consent of the subject.

■ It is lawful to disclose such information if it appears necessary to do so to safeguard a child/ren in the public interest i.e. public interest in protecting children may override public interest in maintaining confidentiality.

■ Disclosure must be justifiable in accordance with the facts of each case and be a proportionate response to the perceived need or risk.

NB. If information is trivial or already in the public domain, there is no breach of confidence when it is

shared e.g. a social worker who was concerned about a child's whereabouts might phone the school to establish if s/he was in school that day.

The approach to confidential information should be the same whether the proposed disclosure is within one or between more than one agency.

- Article 8 of the *European Convention on Human Rights* states that:

  - Everyone has the right to respect for her/his private and family life, home and correspondence
  - There shall be no interference by a public authority with the exercise of this right except in accordance with the law and as is necessary in a democratic society in the interests of national security, public safety or economic well being of the country, for prevention of disorder or crime, for the protection of health or morals, or for the protection of the rights and freedoms of others

- Disclosure of information (appropriate for the purpose and only to the extent that is necessary) **is** justified if it is (as per the criteria in Article 8 above) to:

  - Safeguard a child
  - Protect her/his health or morals
  - Protect the rights and freedoms of others or
  - Prevent disorder or crime

- When disclosing information without consent, the extent of the disclosure must be 'proportionate' to

the need, i.e. disclosure must be limited to that which is absolutely necessary to achieve the aim of the disclosure.

■ The *Data Protection Act 1998* (DPA 1998) as amended requires that personal information is:

- Obtained and processed fairly and lawfully
- Processed for limited purposes and not in any manner incompatible with those purposes
- Accurate and relevant
- Held for no longer than necessary
- Kept secure
- Only disclosed in appropriate circumstances

■ Legitimate conditions (in Schedule 2 of the DPA 1998) for sharing information include that:

- Consent of the person to whom the data relates has been obtained
- Disclosure is necessary to comply with a legal obligation
- It is necessary to protect the vital interests of the data subject
- It is necessary for the exercise of a statutory function or other public function exercised in the public interest e.g. a s.17 assessment or s.47 enquiries and
- It is necessary for the purposes of legitimate interests pursued by the person sharing the information (except where it is unwarranted by reason of prejudice to the rights and freedoms or legitimate interests of the data subject)

NB. The amendments to the DPA 1998 introduced by the Freedom of Information Act 2000 mean that any incidental personal information held in loose papers etc, as opposed to a structured filing system, is now also covered by subject access and accuracy obligations.

■ *'Caldicott'* principles and processes offer a framework of quality standards for the management within health and local authorities of personal information.

■ Health and social services must ensure that their information sharing practices are compliant with HSC/LAC 2002/003/LAC (2002) 2 'Implementing the Caldicott Standards into Social Care'.

NB. Each health and Children's Social Care organisation should have a named 'Caldicott guardian' who can provide advice. A new Caldicott manual was published in March 2010 and can be accessed via www.dh.gov.uk

Professional Guidance for Doctors

■ The General Medical Council (GMC) guidance entitled *Confidentiality: Protecting and Providing Information* (2004) can be found at www.gmc-uk.org/guidance/library/confidentiality.asp

■ The guidance emphasises the importance in most circumstances of obtaining a patient's consent to the disclosure of personal information but makes clear that information may be released (without consent)

to 3rd parties e.g. statutory agencies such as Children's Social Care and Police, if:

- A failure to disclose information may expose the patient, or others, to risk of death or serious harm.

■ The GMC has confirmed that its guidance refers to information about:

- 3rd parties who are of direct relevance to child protection, e.g. adults who may pose a risk to a child
- Children who may be the subject of abuse

Professional Guidance for Nurses & Other Health Staff

■ The Nursing and Midwifery Council (NMC) has produced its *Code of Professional Conduct: Standards for Conduct, Performance and Ethics* (2004) at www. nmc-uk.org/aframedisplay.aspx?documentID=201

■ The above guidance indicates that disclosure of information may occur:

- With the consent of the patient or client
- Without the consent of the patient or client when disclosure is required by law or by court order
- Without the consent of the patient or client when the disclosure is considered to be necessary in the public interest (public interest is defined to include child protection)

Professional Guidance for Police Forces

■ Police are lawfully able to supply information to relevant third parties for defined categories of request.

■ Care must be taken to ensure all information disclosed is accurate, topical, factual, proportionate for the purpose for which it is passed and above all, relevant and necessary to the issue and the individual concerned

■ The categories of request for information which Police can lawfully respond to are those in which:

• A child protection referral is made and a joint investigation under s.47 CA 1989 begun
• Information is requested as part of an inter-agency risk management meeting set up under the SOA 2003
• Children's Social Care is carrying out a s.47 CA 1989 enquiry on a single agency basis
• Children's Social Care is carrying out an initial or core assessment in order to inform a decision as to the justification for a s.47 enquiry
• Children's Social Care is carrying out a 'child in need' assessment under s.17 CA 1989 and written consent from the subject has been obtained or the need to safeguard a child overrides the duty of confidence
• The request relates to a child who is the subject of a child protection plan

- Children's Social Care is faced with an immediate need to place a child with a family member or friend in an emergency and has obtained the necessary consents

■ Information must be provided by the Police on the strict understanding it is confidential in nature, will be used only for purposes of a child protection/in need assessments and may not be passed on to any 3rd party without the express permission of the Police.

Professional Guidance for Education Staff

■ DfES Circular 0027/04 made it clear that education staff had a professional responsibility to share information about the protection of children with other professionals, particularly Police and Children's Social Care.

■ Further explicit obligations of LEAs, schools etc introduced by ss.175 and 157 EA 2002 are laid out on pp.44 above.

Professional Guidance for Social Workers

■ The General Social Care Council (GSCC) and the British Association of Social Workers (BASW) 2002 Code of Ethics allow for divulging confidential information without consent of the service user or informant when there is:

- Clear evidence of serious danger to the service user, worker or other persons

Summary of Law & Professional Guidance with Respect to Information Sharing

■ In general, neither law or professional guidance prevents a professional sharing relevant information with another practitioner if:

  • Those likely to be affected, consent
  • The public interest in safeguarding the child's welfare overrides the need to keep the information confidential
  • Seeking permission might place the child at increased risk of significant harm or
  • Such action might reasonably assist in the prevention or detection of serious crime
  • Disclosure is required by a court order

Agency Checks

■ The consent of a parent or other person with parental responsibility must ordinarily be sought on those occasions when there is a need to gather further information via checks with other agencies, in order to:

  • Progress a s.17 assessment of need
  • Decide whether to re-designate a s.17 assessment of need to a s.47 enquiry or
  • Inform a s.47 enquiry

■ Such checks may be completed without the above consents (in both s.17 and s.47 scenarios) if:

- Seeking consent is believed likely to increase the perceived risk to the child/ren concerned or
- A request for consent has been refused and sufficient professional concern remains to justify such action

Record Keeping

■ Clear and accurate records are essential to effective multi-agency working and provide:

- A documented account of individual and agency involvement
- Continuity when an individual worker changes or is unavailable
- A tool for managers to monitor or peers to review work
- A source of information for enquiries
- Evidence in case of a court hearing

■ All agencies must have policies and arrangements for safe retention and prompt retrieval of records.

■ Records must be clear and concise and differentiate between:

- Fact
- Opinion
- Judgements and
- Hypothesis

■ It should be possible to track from the records kept (usually by Children's Social Care):

- The relevant history of the child/family which led to the intervention
- The nature of interventions, including intended outcomes
- Methods by which change is to be achieved and
- Progress being made

Supervision

- All those involved in child protection should have access to advice and support from peers, managers, named and designated professionals.

- Supervision should scrutinise and evaluate work and case records include key decisions reached during supervision.

SUPPLEMENTARY GUIDANCE

Introduction

■ Chapter 6 *of Working Together to Safeguard Children* 2010 and appx.5 provides some supplementary guidance relevant to specific circumstances summarised (in alphabetical order) below.

Abuse of Disabled Children

- In 2010 the Government published *Safeguarding Disabled Children – Practice Guidance* -see www.dcsf. gov.uk/everychildmatters/download/?=6195

- Available UK evidence suggests disabled children are at increased risk of abuse and neglect and presence of multiple disabilities appears to further increase the risk (see Standards 5, 7 and 8 of the National Standards Framework for Children, Young People and Maternity Services).

- Some may be at increased risk because they:

  - Have fewer outside contacts than other children
  - Receive intimate personal care, possibly from a number of carers
  - Have impaired capacity to resist or avoid abuse
  - Have communication difficulties which may make it difficult to tell others what is happening
  - Are inhibited about complaining for fear of losing services
  - Are especially vulnerable to bullying and intimidation by adults or peers

NB. Looked after disabled children are not only vulnerable to the same factors that exist for all children living away from home, but are particularly susceptible to possible abuse because of their additional dependency on residential or hospital staff day to day physical care needs.

■ Safeguards for disabled children are essentially the same as for all children. Where the child lives or has short breaks away from home, also see p.138). Measures should enable and/or ensure disabled children:

- Make their wishes and feelings known
- Receive appropriate personal, health and social education
- Know how to raise concerns
- Have close contact with families

■ Providers of services for disabled children should have:

- An explicit commitment to, and understanding of, disabled children's safety and welfare
- A culture of openness and
- Guidelines and training for staff in good practice in intimate care; working with children of the opposite sex; handling difficult behaviour; consent to treatment; anti-bullying strategies; sexuality and sexual behaviour among young people, especially those living away from home

■ Special attention should be paid to the child's communication needs, availability of appropriate communication systems (including non verbal) and the use of suitable interpreters or facilitators.

■ When in the child's best interests and the interests of justice, the child should be helped and supported to participate in the criminal justice process. Guidance for investigators is provided in *Achieving Best*

Evidence (2002) at www.cps.gov.uk/publications/
prosecution/bestevidencev012.html

Allegations of Abuse Against Those Working with Children

■ LSCB agencies must, and other agencies providing services to children should, have explicit procedures for handling allegations, consistent with the guidance in appendix 5 of *Working Together to Safeguard Children* 2010.

Roles & Responsibilities

■ LSCB member organisations should have a named senior officer with responsibility for ensuring the organisation operates appropriate procedures, inter-agency issues and liaison with the LSCB.

■ County level and unitary local authorities should also designate officers to:

   • Be involved in management of individual cases
   • Provide advice and guidance to employers and voluntary organisations
   • Liaise with Police and other agencies
   • Monitor cases to ensure they are dealt with expeditiously as possible, consistent with a thorough and fair process

■ Police Forces should identify a senior officer to have strategic oversight of arrangements, liaise with the relevant LSCBs and ensure compliance.

■ Other police officers e.g. unit managers, will have operational responsibility for cases and for liaison with the county/unitary authority designated officer.

Scope of Required Procedures

■ The LSCB procedures apply where there are allegations about a person who works/has worked with children, in connection with her/his current or past work.

■ Procedures should cover all those who work/ed with children, including permanent and temporary employees, agency staff, foster carers, childminders, volunteers and consultants.

■ The criteria for consideration of allegations under this procedure are that the person has:

- Behaved in a way that has/may have harmed a child or
- Possibly committed a criminal offence against or related to a child or
- Behaved towards a child in a way which indicates s/he is unsuitable to work with children

■ All allegations should be followed up regardless of whether the person involved resigns her/his post, responsibilities or position of trust.

General Principles

■ The county or unitary local authority's designated officer should be informed of all allegations that

come to the employer's attention and appear to meet the criteria.

■ An allegation should be tested against the need for:

- Criminal investigation
- A child protection enquiry
- Disciplinary or regulatory response or
- Investigation as a complaint

■ The common facts of alleged abuse must be applied independently to each of the possible responses i.e. the fact that prosecution is not possible does not mean that action in relation to safeguarding children or employee discipline is not necessary or feasible.

■ The child/ren concerned should receive appropriate support. They and their parents/carers should be helped to understand the process and the outcomes, so long as this does not impede the enquiry or disciplinary or investigative processes.

■ The individual about whom there are concerns should, following consultation with police and other relevant agencies, be provided with support, helped to understand the concerns expressed and the process operated. S/he should be clearly informed of the outcome of any investigation and the implications for disciplinary or related processes.

■ If an allegation is substantiated, the managers or commissioners of the service should consider the lessons of the case, including features of the organisation which may have contributed to, or failed

to prevent, the abuse occurring. A serious case review may be appropriate in some cases (see p.63).

Child Abuse linked to 'Spirit Possession'

■ The belief in 'possession' or 'witchcraft' is relatively widespread and not confined to particular countries, cultures, religions or immigrant communities.

■ The children involved:

- Can suffer damage to their physical and mental health, capacity to learn, ability to form relationships and self esteem
- May be perceived as being different or difficult, and attribute this to them being possessed or involved in witchcraft
- May undergo attempts to exorcise them, which may involve severe beatings, burning, starvation, cutting or stabbing and/or isolation – usually within the child's household

■ Agencies should look for possible indicators and apply basic safeguarding principles including information sharing across agencies, in order to be able to identify children at risk of this type of abuse.

NB. Good practice guidance can be found in Safeguarding Children from Abuse Linked to a Belief in Spirit Possession (2007) at www.dcsf.gov.uk/ everychildmatters/download/?id=661

Child Victims of Trafficking

■ Trafficking in people involves a collection of crimes, spanning a variety of countries and involving an increasing number of victims, who experience considerable suffering.

■ Trafficking of children includes:

- Exploitation through force, coercion, threat e.g. prostitution and other forms of sexual exploitation, labour exploitation (including domestic service, sweatshop and restaurant work), begging, picking pockets, benefit fraud, drug mules, trade in human organs
- Use of deception and human rights abuses e.g. debt bondage, deprivation of liberty and lack of control over one's labour

■ The UK is a transit and destination country for trafficked children and young people. Children may enter the UK by various means including as unaccompanied asylum seekers, students or as visitors. They may be brought in by adults who state they are their dependents or met at the airport by an adult claiming to be their relative.

■ If it suspected that a child is the victim of trafficking, the Police or Children's Social Care should be informed. The Trafficking Toolkit (www. crimereduction.gov.uk/toolkits/) provides helpful guidance.

■ The DCSF and Home Office published joint guidance on Safeguarding children who may have been trafficked in 2007 see http://publications. everychildmatters.gov.uk/default.aspx?PageFunction =productdetails&PageMode=publications&ProductId =HMG-00994–2007&

Children Affected by Gang Activity

■ Children and young people who become involved in gangs are at risk of violent crime and as a result are deemed vulnerable.

■ Risks include access to weapons, including knives and firearms, retaliatory and sexual violence, substance misuse and territorial violence with other gangs

■ *Safeguarding Children and Young People who may be affected by gang activity* at http://publications. everychildmatters.gov.uk/default.aspx?PageFunction +productdetails&PageMode=publications&ProductId =DCSF-00064–2010 promotes an approach whereby local agencies should work together to:

  · Clearly define the local problem
  · Understand the risks posed by local gangs
  · Effectively identify young people at risk
  · Assess the needs of children, young people and their families
  · Identify effective referral pathways
  · Support professionals in delivering effective interventions and
  · Define the role of the LSCB and other agencies

Complex (Organised or Multiple) Abuse

■ Complex (organised or multiple) abuse may be defined as abuse involving one or more abuser and a number of children. Abusers may be acting in concert, in isolation or using an institutional framework or position of authority to recruit children for abuse.

■ Complex abuse can occur in families, residential settings, day care, youth services, sports clubs, voluntary groups and via the use of the internet.

■ *Complex Child Abuse Investigations: Inter-Agency Issues* DH & HO May 2002 (found at http://police. homeoffice.gov.uk/news-and-publications/ publication/operational-policing/child_abuse_ guidance.pdf?view=Standard&pubID=184109) provides guidance about the special measures which may be required e.g. formation of dedicated strategic management and investigation teams.

Fabricated or Induced Illness (FII)

■ Fabricated or induced illness in a child is a condition whereby a child suffers harm through the deliberate action of her/his main carer and which is duplicitously attributed by the adult to another cause.

■ The condition may be suggested when a parent or carer of a small child:

• Fabricates signs and symptoms including past medical history and/or
• Falsifies medical charts, records, letters and documents and specimens and/or
• Induces illness by a variety of means

■ Harm to the child may be caused through unnecessary and invasive medical treatment based upon symptoms falsely described or deliberately manufactured by the parent/carer and not independently corroborated.

■ The child may additionally suffer emotional harm through limitations placed on their development and social interaction.

■ *'Safeguarding Children in Whom Illness is Fabricated or Induced'* DH 2008 provides advice at *www.dcsf. gov.uk/everychildmatters/download/?id=3161*

Female Genital Mutilation (FGM)

- The Female Genital Mutilation Act 2003 (in force from 03.03.04 repealed and re-enacted the Prohibition of Female Circumcision Act 1985) and makes female circumcision, excision or infibulation an offence, except on specific health grounds.

- The Act makes it an offence for UK nationals or permanent UK residents to carry out FGM abroad or to aid, abet, counsel or procure the carrying out of FGM abroad, even in countries where the practice is legal.

- A local authority may need to invoke s.47 CA 1989 if it appears a child is likely to become the subject of FGM.

- It may not though, be appropriate to consider removing a child from an otherwise loving family environment and *Working Together to Safeguard Children* 2010 suggests that consideration should be given to obtaining a 'Prohibited Steps Order' if a child appears to be in immediate danger of mutilation (see CAE's companion guide to the Children Act 1989 for further details of this and other s.8 orders).

- In those areas which contain minority ethnic groups known to practice FGM, the LSCB policy should focus on a preventive strategy including community education.

  NB. Further information in support of these guidelines may be found in Local Authority Social Services Letter LASSL (2004)4 at www.dcsf.gov.uk

Forced Marriage

■ A forced marriage is one conducted without the full consent of both parties and where duress is a factor.

■ There is no specific criminal offence of a forced marriage, but forced marriages of children (and vulnerable adults) may involve one or more criminal offences e.g. common assault, cruelty to persons under 16, child abduction, rape, kidnapping, false imprisonment and even murder (see also domestic violence p.144).

■ Attempts at mediation can be extremely dangerous for the child. Concerns should be discussed with the Government's Forced Marriage Unit caseworkers (www.fco.gov.uk 0207 008 0151) and the Police and Children's Social Care contacted.

■ There is further guidance at www.adss.org.uk/ publications/guidance/marriage.pdf ; www.acpo. police.uk/asp/policies/Data/Interactive_Forced_ Marriage 2005.pdf and publications.teachernet.gov. uk/eOrderingDownload/FCO%2075263.pdf

NB. 'Honour crime, 'izzat' or 'honour based' violence are sometimes linked to forced marriage.

Sexually Exploited Children

- Children involved in prostitution and other forms of commercial sexual exploitation should be treated primarily as victims of abuse and their needs assessed.

- 'Safeguarding Children and Young People from Sexual Exploitation DCSF 2009 at *www.dcsf.gov.uk/ everychildmatters/_download/?id=6021* offers guidance.

VULNERABILITY

Introduction

■ Chapter 11 of *Working Together to Safeguard Children* 2010 provides non-statutory practice guidance which is intended to inform the application of standard child protection procedures. An alphabetical summary follows.

Abuse by Children & Young People

Peer Abuse

■ Children, particularly those living away from home, are vulnerable to physical, sexual and emotional bullying and abuse by their peers.

■ Peer abuse should always be taken as seriously as abuse perpetrated by an adult and subject to the same safeguarding procedures.

■ Those working with children and carers need clear guidance and training to identify the difference between consenting and abusive sexual behaviour, and abusive behaviours should not be dismissed as 'normal'.

■ Work with children who abuse others should recognise that such children:

- May pose a significant risk of harm to other children and should be held responsible for their behaviour
- Are likely to have considerable needs themselves and may themselves have witnessed or suffered violence, physical or sexual abuse and may have problems within their development
- Are likely to be children in need and some additionally will be suffering or at risk of significant harm

■ Key principles in responding to concerns of peer abuse are:

- The need for a co-ordinated approach for assessment, decision making and case management by youth justice, Children's Social Care, education (including educational psychology) and health (including child and adolescent mental health)
- The needs of the children who abuse others should be considered separately from the needs of their victims
- A multi agency assessment should be carried out in each case, considering potential unmet developmental needs as well as specific needs arising from their behaviour

■ Relevant considerations in assessing a child who abuses another include:

- The nature, extent and context of the abusive behaviours
- The child's development, family and social circumstances
- The need for services, both with regard to the harmful behaviour and other significant needs
- The risks to self and others, including in the household, extended family, school, peer group or wider social network

■ Decisions for local agencies, according to their individual responsibilities (including the Crown Prosecution Service, when relevant) are:

- The most appropriate course of action within the criminal justice system if the child is above the age of criminal responsibility
- Whether the young abuser is considered personally to be at risk of continuing significant harm and should therefore be the subject of a child protection conference
- Whether a multi-agency approach is required if the threshold for a child protection conference is not met i.e. if the child has complex needs
- What plan of action is required to address the needs of the young abuser, detailing the involvement of all relevant agencies

Bullying

■ Bullying is a form of deliberately hurtful behaviour, usually repeated over a period of time, where it is difficult for the victims to defend themselves.

■ It can take many forms, but the 3 main types are *physical* e.g. hitting, kicking, theft, *verbal* e.g. racist or homophobic remarks, threats, name calling and *emotional* e.g. isolating an individual from social activities.

■ The damage inflicted by bullying is often underestimated and can cause considerable distress to children to the extent that it affects their health and development. In the extreme it can cause significant harm, including self-harm.

■ Since 1999 schools have been under a legal duty to put measures in place to promote good behaviour, respect for others and to prevent all forms of bullying among pupils.

■ All settings in which children are provided with services or are living away from home should have in place rigorously enforced anti-bullying strategies.

■ The DSCF has produced a comprehensive suite of guidance for schools under the title *Safe to Learn: Embedding Anti-bullying Work in Schools* – see http://publicationms.teachernet.gov.uk/default.aspx ?PageFunction=productdetails&PageMode=publicati ons&ProductId=DCSF-00668–2007

Children's Behaviour Indicating a Lack of Parental Control

- Whenever the behaviour of a child brings them to the attention of the Police or the wider community it may indicate vulnerability, poor supervision or the possibility of neglect.

- Consideration should be given to the possibility that the child is 'in need' and should be provided with multi-agency services that reflect her/his need.

- When engagement cannot be secured on a voluntary basis and where a child has committed an act which would have been an offence if s/he were aged 10 or above and where it is necessary to prevent such an act, or where the child has caused harassment, distress or harm to others, a local authority can apply for a Child Safety Order (CSO).

- This compulsory intervention is designed to help the child improve her/his behaviour and is likely to be used alongside work with the family where the child is not assessed as being at risk of significant harm.

- A Parenting Order can be made alongside a CSO, or when a CSO is breached to provide an effective means of engaging with and supporting parents. A Parenting Order consists of 2 elements:

  - A requirement on the parent to attend counselling or guidance sessions e.g. parenting

education or parenting support classes (lasts 3 months)

- A requirement on the parent to comply with such requirements as are determined necessary by the court (up to 12 months)

Child Abuse & Information Communication Technology (ICT)

■ The internet has become a significant tool in the distribution of abusive images of children. As technology develops, the internet and its range of content services can be accessed through various devices.

■ There is a growing concern that children may be abused through:

- Taking, downloading and/or distribution of abusive images of child/ren
- Allowing/encouraging a child to have sustained exposure to inappropriate material via ICT e.g. adult pornography and/or extreme forms of obscene material
- Children engaging in text bullying and use of mobile camera phones to capture violent assaults of other children for circulation

■ Abusive images may be found in the possession of those who use them for personal use or distributed to children as part of the grooming process.

■ Internet chat rooms, discussion forums and bulletin boards are used as a means of contacting children with a view to grooming them for inappropriate/abusive relationships. Subsequent communication may be via e-mail, instant messaging, mobile phone or text message.

- Whenever somebody is discovered to have been involved in the creation, distribution or possession of abusive images of children, the Police should consider the possibility that the individual might also be involved in the active abuse of children and her/his access to children should be established, including family and work settings.

- As part of their role in preventing abuse and neglect, LSCB's should consider activities to raise awareness about the safe use of the internet and be a key partner in the development and delivery of training and education programmes with the Child Education and Online Protection Centre (CEOP). See www.ceop.gov.uk .

  CEOP has also set up its own website which has been designed and written specifically for young people. It contains games and up to date information on having fun, staying in control and being safer online as well as details on how to report problems. See www.ceop.gov.uk/children_and_young_people.asp.

Children of Families Living in Temporary Accommodation

■ Placement in temporary accommodation, often at a distance from previous support networks, can lead to individuals and families falling through the net and becoming disengaged from health, education, social and welfare support systems.

■ Some families who have experienced homelessness and are placed in temporary accommodation by local authorities in response to their homelessness duties can have very transient lifestyles.

■ Some families in which children are harmed move home frequently avoiding contact with caring agencies so that no single agency has a complete picture of the family.

Children & Families whose Whereabouts are Unknown

- Local agencies and professionals must consider, with respect to a child about whom there are concerns (including where there are concerns about an unborn child who may be at future risk of significant harm) that a series of missed appointments or abortive home visits may indicate that the family has moved out of the area.

- In the above circumstances, both Children's Social Care and Police must be notified as soon as such concerns arise and will need to initiate enquiries.

- Consideration may need to be given to legal action if it appears that a child, for whom there are outstanding protection concerns, may be removed from the UK to avoid protection agencies.

- The Consular Directorate of the Foreign and Commonwealth Office offers assistance to British nationals in distress overseas (www.fco.gov.uk 020 7008 1500) and for children taken overseas may be able to follow up concerns through consular post/s in the relevant country.

- If a child who is subject to a Care Order is removed from the UK, Children's Social Care, the police and the Child Abduction Section of the Foreign and Commonwealth Office should be immediately informed.

- When looked after children run away or go missing, local procedures/protocols should be followed and it is important to understand the reasons that may have contributed to their going missing.

- Children missing from education could be at risk of significant harm and every practitioner working with the child has a responsibility to inform the local Child Missing Education (CME) contact in the local authority if they know or suspect a child is not receiving education – see Identifying and maintaining contact with children missing, or at risk of going missing, from education DfES 2004 www.everychildmatters.gov.uk/ ete/?asset=document&id=15394

Children Living Away From Home

- Children living away from home are vulnerable to all sexual and physical abuse, emotional abuse and neglect, including peer abuse, bullying and substance misuse.

- The circumstances include boarding schools, children's homes, placement with foster carers, private fostering, hospitals, prisons, young offender institutions, secure training centres, secure units, army bases, foreign students and foreign exchange visits.

- A variety of safeguards can reduce risk of abuse/ neglect:

  - Children feeling valued and respected, being listened to and their wishes, feelings, views and concerns ascertained
  - An openness to the external world, including families and community
  - Ready access by children to trusted adults
  - Clear, accessible and effective complaints procedures
  - Rigorous recruitment and selection procedures
  - Staff/carers trained in all aspects of safeguarding children
  - Effective supervision and support extending to temporary staff and volunteers
  - Clear procedures and support systems for referring concerns by children and by staff or

carers which do not prejudice any 'whistle-blowers' own position and prospects (see p.?? Allegations against Those Working with Children & p.?? Abuse by Children)

- Strategies to effectively counter bullying
- A respect for diversity and sensitivity to race, religion, gender, sexuality and disability
- Social workers regular visits to looked after children and those that are privately fostered, seeing the child alone (taking appropriate account of the child's wishes and feelings)

■ S.118 ACA 2002 requires a local authority to appoint an independent reviewing officer to participate in and monitor effectiveness of reviews of looked after children. This officer can refer a case to an officer of the CAFCASS (CAFCASS Cymru in Wales) if s/he considers it appropriate to do so, and that officer will be empowered to apply to return the case to court.

■ The local authority's duty to undertake s.47 enquiries applies on the same basis to children living away from home as it does to children who live with their own families.

Private Fostering

■ Under the CA 1989, private foster carers and those with parental responsibility are required to notify the local authority of their intention to privately foster/ have a child privately fostered.

- Other professionals should notify Children's Social Care of a private fostering arrangement that comes to their attention.

- Amendments to s.67 and Sch.8 CA 1989 (made by s.44 of the CA 2004) require local authorities to promote awareness of notification requirements.

- The Children (Private Arrangements for Fostering) Regulations 2005 require the local authority to satisfy itself of the suitability of a proposed arrangement *before* it commences (where advance notice is given) i.e. of the suitability of the private foster carer, carer's household and accommodation.

- The local authority has the power to impose requirements on the private foster carer or, if there are serious concerns about an arrangement, to prohibit it.

- The CA 1989 creates a number of offences including failure to:

  - Notify a private foster care arrangement or
  - Comply with any requirement or prohibition imposed by the local authority

- CA 1989 guidance on private fostering, issued in July 2005 (reflecting the new measures in the CA 2004) and the National Minimum Standards for private fostering are available at www.dcsf.gov.uk/ everychildmatters/dowlnload/?id=2596

Children in Hospital

■ *The National Service Framework for Children, Young People and Maternity Services* (NSF) 2004 requires hospitals to ensure their facilities are secure and regularly reviewed.

■ The local authority where the hospital is located is responsible for the welfare of child patients.

■ Children should not be cared for on an adult ward. The NSF standard for Hospital Services requires care to be in an appropriate location and an environment that is safe and appropriate for the child's age and stage of development.

■ S.85 CA 1989 requires PCTs to notify the 'responsible authority' i.e. the local authority for the area in which the child is ordinarily resident or where accommodated if unclear, when a child has been or will be accommodated by the PCT for 3 months or more, so that the local authority can assess the child's needs.

Youth Justice System

■ In fulfilling their statutory function of reducing offending and re-offending by children and young people, YOTs have dual responsibilities in the area of safeguarding as well as public protection including the protection of other children and young people.

■ Those sentenced or remanded in custody are among he most vulnerable and required in addition the

establishment's day to day care ongoing support from children's services and the LSCB.

■ Functions, powers, duties, responsibilities and obligations imposed on local authorities by the Children Act 1989 e.g. s.17 and s.47 do not cease to arise because a child is in the secure estate. They operate subject to the requirements of imprisonment.

■ If a looked after child who is subject of a Care Order enters a YOI on sentence or remand, the responsible authority has continuing responsibilities as a corporate parent to visit and continue to asses their needs/revierw their case/facilitate contact with family etc.

■ If a child under 16 who has been accommodated under s.20 CA 1989 i.e. voluntarily, enters custody, s/he ceases to be looked after.

■ Planned regulations under s.15 Children and Young Persons' Act 2008 will require a responsible local authority to ensure that it appoints a representative to visit all children and young people who have ceased to be accommodated. This representative will be responsible for assessing the child's needs in order to make recommendations about the support s/he will need whilst detained and in particular after release e.g. might s/he need to become looked after again ?

■ Children aged 16+ who were looked after prior to be being sentenced may well be 'relevant children' as defined by s.23A Children Act 1989 (as amended by

the Children (Leaving Care) Act 2000. The
responsible authority must appoint a personal adviser
and prepare a pathway plan setting out the support
the authority will provide e.g. identifying where the
child will live on release, the support s/he will
receive so as to minimise the possibility of
re-offending.

Domestic Violence

- The Home Office (*What is Domestic Violence ?* London Home Office 2009) defines domestic violence as 'any incident of threatening behaviour, violence or abuse (psychological, physical, sexual, financial or emotional) between adults who are or have been intimate partners or family members, regardless of gender or sexuality'.

- Prolonged and/or regular exposure to domestic violence can have a serious effect on the development and emotional well being of a child, (including an unborn child whose mother may be punched or kicked in her abdomen).

- Children may suffer harm through being physically hurt during episodes of violence and/or through witnessing the physical assaults and emotional suffering of a parent.

- The serious effects on the child often results in behavioural issues, absenteeism, ill health, bullying, anti-social behaviour, substance misuse, self harm and psychosocial impacts.

- In addition to assessing the impact on a child of observing domestic violence between adult partners, professionals should be alert to the strong link between domestic violence and child abuse.

- When it is believed a child is being abused, those involved with the child and family should also be

alert to the possibility of domestic violence within the family.

- Police are often the first point of contact following domestic violence incidents and when responding should:

  - Establish if any children live in the household
  - See any children present to assess their immediate safety
  - Establish with Children's Social Care if the child/ren are subject to a child protection plan
  - Determine if there are any court orders or injunctions in force in respect of household members
  - Undertake an assessment and make a referral to Children's Social Care if there are any specific concerns about the safety or welfare of any child, clarifying if the family is aware of the referral

- Normally, 1 serious or several lesser incidents of domestic violence when there is a child in the household indicates that Children's Social Care should carry out an initial assessment, including consulting existing records.

- If there is a baby of less than 12 months in the household (including an unborn child), and even if the child was not present, professionals should make a referral to Children's Social Care in the event of even a single incident of domestic violence.

- Children's Social Care response to such referrals should be discreet and not further endanger victims

or children e.g. care should be taken over the use and wording of any letters sent to the household.

■ Existing records should be consulted and an initial assessment should usually be undertaken after one serious or several lesser incidents of domestic violence where there is a child in the household. This should include consideration of any agreed contact arrangements between the child/ren and a non resident parent.

■ The children may benefit from a range of services and some may need safeguarding from harm. Often supporting a non-violent parent is likely to be the most effective way to promote the child/ren's welfare.

Sharing Information

■ Education, early years and health service professionals are well placed to identify domestic violence.

■ Guidance on best practice for health service staff is available in the toolkit *Improving Safety, Reducing harm: Children, young people and domestic violence – a practical toolkit for front line practitioners* –see www.dh.gov.uk/prod_consum_dh/groups/dh_digitalassets/documents/digitalasset/dh_108704.pdf

Learning Disability of Parent/Carer

- Learning disabled parents may need support to develop the understanding, resources, skills and experience to meet the needs of their children.

- Such support is vital if the parent/s experience additional stressors e.g. caring for a disabled child, domestic violence, poor physical or mental health, substance misuse, social isolation, poor housing, poverty or a history of growing up in care.

- Unless the parents are comprehensively supported by a capable non-abusive relative or partner (or alternative provision), the child's health and development is likely to be impaired.

- Adult learning disability services, particularly community nurses, can provide valuable input to core assessments. Validated assessment tools are also available and should be applied as early as possible i.e. pre-birth.

- A specialist assessment may be needed to ensure that crucial decisions are made on adequate information.

Mental Illness of Parent/Carer

■ Most parents who suffer significant mental ill-health are able to care for and safeguard their child/ren and/or unborn child, but it is essential always to assess the implications for each child in the family.

■ In some cases the parent's condition will seriously affect the safety, health and development of children. This applies particularly to enduring and/or severe parental mental ill health or where there is associated family disharmony/break-up or where there is a lack of support from other family members.

■ In the latest such review of serious case reviews reports where children had either died or been seriously harmed, current or past mental illness was found in two thirds of cases – see Brandon M etc *Understanding Serious Case Reviews and their Impact: A biennial Analysis of Serious Case Reviews* 2005–07 London DCSF.

Self Harm

- Self harm, self mutilation, eating disorders, suicide threats and gestures by a child must always be taken seriously and may be indicative of a serious mental or emotional disturbance.

- In most cases of deliberate self harm the young person should be offered help via the school counselling service, the GP, child & adolescent mental health service (CAMHS) or other therapeutic services e.g. paediatric or psychiatric services.

- The possibility that self-harm, including a serious eating disorder, has been caused or triggered by any form of abuse or chronic neglect should not be over-looked and justifies a referral to Children's Social Care.

- Consideration must also be given to protect children who engage in high risk behaviour which may cause serious self injury such as drug or substance misuse, running away, partaking in daring behaviour i.e. running in front of cars etc all of which may indicate underlying behavioural or emotional difficulties or abuse.

- It is good practice, *whenever* a child or young person is known to have either made a suicide attempt or been involved in self harming to undertake a multi-disciplinary risk assessment, along with an assessment of need.

- Younger children e.g. under 12 years should also have a comprehensive paediatric assessment.

Substance Misuse by Parent/Carer

■ Substance misuse may include experimental, recreational, poly-drug, chaotic and dependent use of alcohol and/or drugs.

■ Parental misuse of drugs or alcohol becomes relevant to child protection when the misuse of the substances impacts on the care provided to child/ren or the health and development of an unborn child.

■ The risk will be greater when combined with other features such as domestic violence, mental illness and the children will be particularly vulnerable when parents are withdrawing from drugs.

■ A thorough assessment is required to determine the extent of need and level of risk of harm in every case. This should involve both drug services and Children's Social Care.

Unaccompanied Asylum Seeking Children (UASC)

- A UASC is an asylum-seeking child under the age of 18 who is not living with her/his parent, relative or guardian in the UK.

- In most cases, UASC will be referred to local authorities by the UK Border Agency (UKBA) shortly after they arrive in the UK.

- Local authorities should adopt the same approach to assessing the needs of UASC as used for other children in their area. Because the child will have no parent, relative or other suitable adult carer in the UK, s/he is likely to need to be accommodated under s.20 Children Act 1989.

- In the majority of cases this will lead to them being accommodated under s.20 CA 1989 and subject to a care plan (pathway plan at 16+).

- In assessing the needs of an UASC and providing effective care, local authorities will normally need to build close relationships with the UKBA 'case owner' responsible for resolving the child's immigration status. This should extend to sharing key information necessary to safeguard the child's welfare, including information:

  - Relevant to the assessment of the child's identity and age (given that most UASCs may not have reliable documentary evidence)

- That might be relevant to the immigration decision e.g. if a child has complex medical needs or is suffering from trauma
- About any efforts to trace the location of family members in the country of origin (many UASC have lost contact with family members because of the circumstances of their journey to the UK)

NB. It should not be assumed that an UASC child will remain permanently in the UK unless and until s/he is granted British Nationality, refugee status or indefinite leave to remain. Thus opportunities available in the country of origin should be addressed in the care or pathway plan.

Underage Sexual Activity

■ Most young people under the age of 18 have an interest in sex and sexual relationships. All children and young people should be given appropriate protection from sexual abuse whilst ensuring that they are also able to access advice and treatment about contraception, sexual and reproductive health including abortion.

The Law

■ The minimum legal age for young people of either gender to consent to have sex is 16 years whether they are straight, gay or bisexual.

■ Sexual activity with a child under 16 is an offence. Where it is consensual it may be less serious than if the child were under 13, but may nevertheless have serious consequences for the welfare of the child.

■ Sexual activity with children under 13 is always illegal as children of this age are not legally capable of giving their consent. Under the Sexual Offences Act 2003, penetrative sex with a child under 13 renders the offender liable to imprisonment for life.

■ The Sexual Offences Act 2003 does allow professionals to provide young people (even if they are less than 16 years) with confidential advice on contraception, condoms, pregnancy and abortion, see also *Working within the Sexual Offences Act* Home Office May 2004 SOA/4).

- The above Act states that a person is not guilty of arranging or facilitating a sexual offence against a child where they are acting for the purpose of:

  - Protecting a child from pregnancy or sexually transmitted infection
  - Protecting the physical safety of a child
  - Promoting a child's emotional well-being by the giving of advice

- This exception, in statute, covers not only health professionals, but anyone who acts to protect a child, for example teachers, school nurses, Connexions personal advisers, youth workers, social workers and parents.

Children Under 13 Years of Age

- Where the allegation concerns penetrative sex, or other intimate sexual activity, *Working Together to Safeguard Children* 2010 states 'there would always be reasonable cause to suspect that a child, whether a girl or boy, is suffering or is likely to suffer significant harm. There should be a *presumption* that the case will be reported to Children's Social Care and that a strategy discussion will be held ...'

- All cases involving under 13s must be fully documented, including any detailed reasons where a decision is taken not to share information.

- A decision not to refer should only be made following a case discussion with the designated lead for child protection within the professional's employing

authority. When a referral is not made, the professional and agency concerned are fully accountable for the decision.

Children Aged 13 – 15 Years Inclusive

■ Sexual activity with a child under 16 is an offence. Even where this is consensual it may have serious consequences for the welfare of the child.

■ In every case involving a child aged 13–15, consideration must be given to a discussion with other agencies and whether a referral should be made to Children's Social Care. This decision should be based on the level of risk/need assessed by those working with the young person taking into consideration:

- The age, level of maturity and understanding of the child – the younger the child the stronger the presumption must be that sexual activity is a matter of concern
- Power imbalances, including through age and development – size, gender, sexuality, levels of sexual knowledge
- Where a child has a learning disability or communication difficulty
- Use of overt aggression, coercion or bribery
- Use of alcohol and/or drugs were to facilitate the activity
- If the child's own behaviour e.g. use of drugs means s/he is unable to make an informed choice

- Any attempts to secure secrecy by the sexual partner beyond what is usual in teenage relationships e.g. her/his identity being a secret
- If the sexual partner is known by agencies to have concerning relationships with other children
- If the child denies or minimises adult concerns
- Presence of a sexually transmitted infection in a child
- If the relationship involves behaviours considered to be 'grooming' in the context of sexual exploitation
- Where sex has been used to gain favours e.g. cigarettes, clothes, CDs, trainers, alcohol, drugs etc
- Where the young person has a lot of money/ valuables which cannot be accounted for
- Knowledge of child's circumstances/background
- The child's behaviour e.g. withdrawn, anxious

■ Cases of concern should be discussed with the nominated child protection lead for the agency and subsequently with other agencies if required.

■ Where confidentiality needs to be preserved, a discussion can occur without identifying the child directly or indirectly.

■ Where there is reasonable cause to suspect that significant harm to a child has/might occur, a referral should be made to Children's Social Care and a strategy discussion held.

Child Aged 16 or 17 Years Old

■ Although sexual activity in itself is not an offence once a child attains the age of 16, young people under 18 are still offered the protection of child protection procedures under the CA 1989.

■ Consideration still needs to be given to the following circumstances:

- Issues of sexual exploitation through prostitution and abuse of power
- Offences of rape and assault- the circumstances of an incident may need to be explored with a young person
- 'Abuse of a position of trust' – when a person aged 18 or over commits against the under 18 year old for whom s/he is a position of trust one of a range of offences contained in the Sexual Offences Act 2003 or
- 'Familial child sex offences' also contained in the above Act

Violent Extremism

■ Exposure to, or involvement with groups or individuals who condone violence as means to a political end is a particular risk for some children. They can be drawn into violence themselves or can be exposed to messages if a family member is involved in an extremist group.

■ Levels of risk vary across different areas so LSCBs, safeguarding adult boards and children's services practitioners should ensure they are informed of the particular risks in their area.

■ Most areas have a 'Prevent partnership group' (Prevent is the cross Government strategy to stop people becoming terrorists or supporting violent extremism) that is responsible for co-ordinating work across all agencies.

■ Children's Services should be involved in such partnerships and all children and young peoples' partnerships should have an agreed process in place for safeguarding vulnerable individuals, including transition and vulnerable adult services.

■ In some areas, there is a bespoke multi agency process known as 'Channel' which is an agreed mechanism for referring those at risk and providing support. Channel guidance indicates that if a referred individual is under 18 the Channel co-ordinator must liaise with the CAF co-ordinator or Children's Social Care.

Young Carers

■ A young carer is a young person under 18 who has a responsibility for caring on a regular basis for a relative (or very occasionally a friend) who has an illness or disability. This can be primary or secondary caring and leads to a variety of losses for the young carer.

■ Many young carers experience:

- Low level of school attendance and/or some educational difficulties
- Social isolation
- Conflict between loyalty to family and their wish to have their own needs met

■ It is often difficult to identify young carers because they may remain silent, whilst trying to keep the family together.

■ The problem of identification can be further compounded where there is an able bodied adult/s within the home whom it may be assumed is undertaking all of the care, but may in fact, be working long hours to keep the family financially secure and delegating caring responsibilities to the child.

■ All agencies in contact with young carers should consider if they are in need of support services in their own right and/or if they are at risk of significant harm.

CHILD PROTECTION PROCESSES

Referral of a Child Believed to be At Risk

- The child's immediate safety must be safeguarded and the law allows anyone with actual care of a child e.g. a teacher or a member of health staff to 'do what is reasonable in all the circumstances of the case for the purpose of safeguarding or promoting a child's welfare' [s.3 (5) CA 1989].

- Processes described below should also be followed when there are concerns about the welfare of an unborn baby.

Referral Route

- A referral should generally be made to Children's Social Care covering the child's home address.

- If the above information is unknown a referral should be made to the nearest Children's Social Care.

- Maximum personal information about the child, her/his circumstances and cause/s of concern should be relayed (though a referral must not be delayed to increase the available information).

- Professional referrals to Children's Social Care should be confirmed in writing within 48 hours, using local formats. When a CAF has been completed this should be provided.

■ The referrer should record in writing and sign the time, date and content of her/his discussions or contact with:

- Child
- Parent/s
- Agency manager and
- Children's Social Care

Involvement of Child

■ Where abuse is alleged by a child, the response should be limited to listening carefully to what is said so as to:

- Clarify the concerns
- Offer re-assurance about how s/he will be kept safe and
- Inform her/him what action will be taken

Involvement of Parent/ s/ Carer

■ When possible, concerns should be discussed with the family and agreement sought for a referral to Children's Social Care unless it is concluded the process of discussing the concern may, by delay or the behavioural response it prompts, place the child at increased risk.

■ A decision by any professional not to seek parental permission before making a referral to Children's Social Care must be recorded and the reasons given.

■ The referral to Children's Social Care should make it
clear if the parent or carer has been informed of the
concern and if permission for the referral was
obtained.

Alleged Crimes

■ Whenever Children's Social Care has a case referred
to it which may constitute a criminal offence against
a child, it must be discussed with the Police as soon
as possible.

■ Whenever other agencies, or the local authority in its
other roles, encounter concerns which may constitute
a criminal offence against a child, they must always
consider sharing that information with Children's
Social Care and Police. Any decision not to do so
must be recorded (see p.?? for guidance on underage
sexual activity).

■ The decision about when to inform parents of
referrals should take into account that this will have
a bearing on the conduct of Police investigations.

■ Whilst it is the responsibility of the Police to
investigate alleged or potential crime, they should
consider the views of other agencies and the best
interests of the child (see strategy discussions p.??)

Response of Children's Social Care to a Referral

■ Children's Social Care, having clarified and considered the information provided, the views of other key agencies and any existing records, should decide and record the next steps within 1 working day.

■ The decision should be recorded by Children's Social Care and an acknowledgement provided to referrers within 1 working day of receipt of referral.

■ If a referrer has not received an acknowledgement within 3 working days, s/he should contact Children's Social Care again.

Initial & Core Assessments

■ An 'initial assessment of need' (IA) as described in the '*Framework for the Assessment of Children In Need and Their Families*' DH 2000 should be led by a qualified and experienced social worker, take into account relevant history (including from equivalent services abroad if applicable) and completed within 10 working days of receipt of referral.

■ The process of an IA should involve:

• Seeing and speaking to the child, including alone when appropriate
• Seeing and meeting with parents, family and wider family members as appropriate

- • Involving and obtaining relevant information from professionals and others in contact with the child and family
  - • Drawing together and analysing available information (focusing on the strengths and positive factors as well as vulnerabilities and risk factors) from a range of sources (including agency records)

- ■ Children's Social Care is obliged by the Children Act 1989 as amended by s.53 Children Act 2004 to ascertain the child's wishes and feelings and to give due consideration to them having regard to age and understanding when making decisions about what (if any) services to provide.

- ■ The family, the original referrer and other professionals should ordinarily be informed of the outcome of an IA, consistent with the confidentiality of the child and family concerned, and with further action required in respect of concerns about harm or criminal investigations. The information should be confirmed in writing to the family and other agencies.

- ■ A 'core assessment' (CA) (which should be completed within a further 35 working days) may be justified:

  - • If the initial assessment indicates complex needs
  - • When a strategy discussion initiates a s.47 enquiry
  - • When new information about an open case indicates that its is required

Immediate Protection

■ Where there is a risk to the life of a child or a likelihood of serious immediate harm, rapid action is required and the duties and powers available to Police and Children's Social Care are described on pps.73 and 83.

■ The local authority in which the child is found is responsible for initiating any emergency action.

■ Emergency action will normally take place following an immediate strategy discussion, but where a single agency has to act immediately to protect a child, a strategy discussion should take place as soon as possible after the action to plan the next steps.

Strategy Discussion

■ Whenever there is reasonable cause to suspect that a child is suffering or likely to suffer significant harm, there should be a strategy discussion convened by Children's Social Care involving Police and other agencies as appropriate, in particular any referring agency.

■ The purposes of a strategy discussion are to:

  • Share available information
  • Agree conduct and timing of any criminal
  • Decide whether s.47 enquiries and a CA should be initiated or continued if already in motion
  • Plan how enquiries should be handled, including the need for medical assessment/treatment
  • Agree what immediate action is needed to ensure the child's safety and/or offer services or support
  • Determine the most appropriate timing for parental participation in the enquiry (taking into account the conduct of Police investigations and the child's safety)
  • Determine if legal action is required

■ A strategy discussion may take place by telephone or at a meeting (held in a convenient location for all attendees). A meeting is the most effective in complex types of abuse or neglect.

■ More than 1 strategy discussion may be necessary, where the child's circumstances are complex.

Conduct of s.47 Enquiries

- Enquiries may be conducted by Children's Social Care or Police, alone or jointly.

- When joint enquiries take place, the Police have the lead for the criminal investigation and Children's Social Care the lead for s.47 enquiries.

- Each LSCB should have a protocol to guide both agencies in deciding how s.47 enquiries and associated police investigations should be conducted.

- *The Framework for the Assessment of Children in Need and Their Families* DH 2000 core assessment provides a structure for collection and analysis of information gathered in the course of a s.47 enquiry. The initial focus will be the cause for concern, but the completed core assessment should cover all relevant dimensions in the 'Assessment Framework'.

- Consideration should be given to the potential needs and safety of all children in the household and family, and any other children with whom an alleged offender may have contact.

- Enquiries should include separate interviews with the child/ren who is/are the subject/s of concern and (in the majority of cases) interviews with parents/caregivers and observation of interaction between parents and child/ren.

- Exceptionally a joint enquiry/investigation may need to speak to the suspected child victim without the

knowledge of parent. Relevant circumstances include the possibility that a child would otherwise be threatened or coerced into silence, a strong likelihood that important evidence would be destroyed or that a child in question does not wish the parent to be involved at that stage and is competent to take that decision.

Evidential Video Interviews

■ In accordance with *Achieving Best Evidence in Criminal Proceedings* HO 2007 joint video interviews, involving Police and Children's Social Care, should be conducted by those with specialist training and experience.

■ Criminal justice legislation creates particular obligations for courts dealing with witnesses under 17 years (and planned to rise to 18) , including the presumption of evidence giving through pre-recorded videos, as well as the use of live video links for further evidence-giving and cross examination. Cross-examination in pre-trial video hearings may also occur in relevant cases.

Outcome of Enquiries

■ Children's Social Care should decide how to proceed following s.47 enquiries, after discussion with all those who have been significantly involved in those enquiries.

■ The information recorded on the outcome of s.47 enquiries record should be provided to parents, children of sufficient age and understanding and significantly involved professionals and agencies.

Concerns Not Substantiated

■ The core assessment should be completed where concerns are unsubstantiated and consideration given, with the family, for any support and/or services that may be helpful and any arrangements that may be advisable for monitoring the child's welfare.

Substantiated Concerns & Child Not Judged to Be at Continuing Risk

■ When concerns are substantiated but the child is not judged to be at continuing risk of significant harm the core assessment should be completed and a child in need plan developed (involving professionals and family members) to provide further support.

■ A meeting of involved professionals and family members may be helpful to agree actions and

planned outcomes. Family Group Conferences (FGCs) may have a role in fulfilling the tasks.

■ In these circumstances a senior manager or named or designated professionals in agencies involved in the s.47 enquiry have the right to request that Children's Social Care convene a child protection conference if they have serious concerns that a child's welfare may not otherwise be adequately safeguarded. This request should normally be agreed.

Substantiated Concerns & Child Judged to Be at Continuing Risk

■ Where the concerns are substantiated and the child is judged to be at continuing risk of significant harm a child protection conference should be convened.

Initial Conference

■ An initial child protection conference must be convened no later than 15 working days following the (or last of the) strategy discussion/s.

■ Purposes of initial child protection conferences (which bring together family members, child (when appropriate), supporters/advocates and involved professionals) are to:

- Collate and analyse in an inter-agency setting the information gathered about a child's health, development and functioning, parent/s' capacity to ensure the child's safety and promote her/his health and development
- Make judgements about the likelihood and continuing risk of a child suffering significant harm in the future
- Decide what future action is needed to safeguard the child and promote her/his welfare, how that action will be taken forward and with what intended outcomes
- Allocate a lead social worker for children made subject of child protection plans
- (When relevant) identify a multi-agency core group to develop and monitor the outline child protection plan

■ Before the conference the purpose and operation of the meeting should be explained to the child of

sufficient age, the parent/s and involved family members and their involvement carefully planned.

NB. Failure to involve the family properly in such a meeting may result in an action for breach of human rights under Articles 6 and 8 see e.g. R v UK [1988] 2 FLR 445; and the decision of the Court of Appeal in Re S and Re W [2001] 2 FLR 582, which was untouched on these points in relation to the possibility of actions based on human rights claims. Also see Re M (Care : Challenging Decisions by Local Authority) [2001] 2 FLR 1300 where the local authority had reached decisions about the child in a crisis meeting which the parents did not attend because they did not know it was being held, which was deemed by the court to be a breach of Article 8.

Actions & Decisions of the Conference

- If the child is judged to be at continuing risk of significant harm by the conference, inter-agency help and intervention should be provided by a formal child protection plan.

- The decision must take account of the views of all agencies represented at the conference and any written contributions. The method used should be set out in local LSCB procedures/protocol.

- The chairperson should determine the category of abuse or neglect the child has suffered or is at risk of suffering.

■ The conference should establish time scales, outline the child protection plan and a contingency plan if agreed actions are not completed.

■ When a child is not to be the subject of a child protection plan, the conference should consider her/ his needs, what further help should be provided and if a child in need plan should be drawn up.

Pre-Birth Conference

■ A pre-birth initial conference may be held when there is a need to consider whether (usually following a pre-birth assessment) an inter-agency protection plan is required.

■ A pre-birth conference should be held where an assessment gives rise to concerns that an unborn child may be at future risk of significant harm.

■ Circumstances that should be subject to a pre-birth assessment include where:

• A previous child has died or been removed from parent/s as a result of significant harm
• A child is to be born into a household which already has child/ren subject to child protection plan/s
• A parent or other adult in the household (or a regular visitor) is a person identified as presenting a risk, or potential risk, to children
• There is a knowledge of parental risk factors e.g. substance misuse, mental illness, domestic violence, self-care issues

Implementing Child Protection Plan

- The lead social worker has the lead role for making sure the outline plan at the initial conference is developed into a more detailed inter-agency plan, securing contributions from family and core group members as necessary.

- The core group is responsible for working with the lead social worker to develop and implement the detailed child protection plan.

- The first meeting of the core group should be within 10 working days of the initial child protection conference and subsequent meetings held sufficiently regularly to facilitate working together, monitoring actions and outcomes and making any changes to the plan as circumstances change.

Review Conference

■ The purposes of review conferences (the first of which must be held within 3 months of the initial conference and thereafter at intervals of not more than 6 months) are to:

- Review whether the child is continuing to suffer or likely to suffer significant harm and her/his health and developmental of the child with respect to the planned outcomes set out in the child protection plan
- Ensure that the child continues to be safeguarded from harm
- Consider whether the child protection plan should continue or should be changed

Complaints About Conferences

- Parents, carers or a child (considered by chairperson to have sufficient understanding) may make a complaint to the conference chairperson in respect of one of the following aspects of conferences:

  - Process employed
  - Outcome, in terms of fact of and/or category of primary concern
  - Decision for the child to become/not to become subject of a child protection plan or not to cease being subject of such a plan

- Paras.5.107 to 5.110 of *Working Together to Safeguard Children* 2010 offer guidance on the management of complaints and indicate that new regulations are anticipated.

APPENDICES

Appendix 1: Consent & Refusal of Medical Assessment or Treatment

General Principles

- The consent (of a parent with parental responsibility, patient her/himself or of a court) is a necessary prerequisite for treatment of all under 18 year olds.

  NB. The effect of consent is to protect the practitioner from a claim in trespass/charge of assault.

- In an emergency a doctor is lawfully entitled to undertake such treatment as appears necessary to safeguard the life and health of a patient until such time as consent can be sought from one of the above sources.

Consent of a Competent Minor of 16 or 17 Years of Age

- A minor of 16 or 17 has a specific right to give consent to surgical, medical or dental treatment [s.8 FLRA 1969].

- Unless grounds exist for believing that s/he might be mentally incompetent within the meaning of the MHA 1983 no further consent is required.

  NB. This right does not extend to the donation of blood or organs.

■ A person who has parental responsibility for a young person of this age cannot override her/his consent (cf.- refusal below).

Consent by a Competent Minor of Less than 16 Years of Age

■ A child (of any age) who has 'sufficient understanding to make an informed decision' is able to give a valid consent to treatment.

■ A judgement as to the child's level of understanding would normally be for the doctor (in consultation with others as necessary) to form, and the degree of understanding needed would of course be greater, the more complicated the treatment.

NB. The consent of an under 16 year old who has sufficient understanding cannot be overridden by a person with parental responsibility.

Refusal of Treatment by a Minor of Any Age

■ The Court of Appeal has expressed the view that a consent from someone who has parental responsibility would legitimise treatment of an unwilling minor of 16 or 17, or an under 16 year old of 'sufficient understanding'.

NB. The consent of only one person who has parental responsibility is required.

Refusal by Persons with Parental Responsibility and a Competent Minor

■ Where those with parental responsibility and a competent child are not prepared to give consent it would be necessary to invoke the inherent jurisdiction of the High Court so it could provide the necessary consent.

■ Where the local authority has parental responsibility by virtue of a Care or interim Care Order, it could provide consent to proposed medical treatment.

■ If, parent/s or others with parental responsibility were unwilling to consent, the local authority would be obliged to seek a court order to authorise it [South Glamorgan County Council v A & B 1993 2 FLR].

Refusal by Those with Parental Responsibility of Treatment for a Child Not Considered 'Competent'

■ If there is no one with parental responsibility who is prepared to give the necessary consent and the child is not considered competent, an application can be made to:

  • A court for a Specific Issue Order
  • The High Court to exercise its inherent jurisdiction to grant leave to administer the proposed treatment

■ The court's decision will override any objection by the child or others with parental responsibility.

- If there is insufficient time to make such an application Ministry of Health guidance F/P9/1B and Home Office Circular 63/1968 should be followed.

- These suggest that a consultant may give treatment if s/he has had a full discussion with parents, obtained written support from a colleague to the effect that the child's life is in danger if treatment is withheld and an acknowledgement from the parents that in spite of the risk, they are still refusing their consent.

- Also as a matter of common law, where a doctor decides in an emergency to take any necessary steps to save the life of a child, it is not possible to take any legal action against her/him arising from that decision (unless s/he can be shown to have been negligent).

Specific Rights of Child to Refuse Assessment or Treatment

- The Children Act 1989 in theory, provides that a child who is subject to the following Orders and who has 'sufficient understanding to make an informed decision' has a specific right to refuse medical or psychiatric examination or any other form of assessment:

  - Interim Supervision or interim Care Order [s.38(6) CA 1989]
  - Child Assessment Order [s.43(8) CA 1989]

- Emergency Protection Order [s.44(7) CA 1989]
- Supervision Order [Sch.3 Para.4 CA 1989]

■ It has now been made clear in a series of cases that such refusals can be overridden by an Order of the High Court using its inherent jurisdiction [South Glamorgan County Council v A & B 2 FLR 1993].

■ In the case of interim Supervision and interim Care Orders, Child Assessment Orders and Emergency Protection Orders, the judgement of 'sufficient understanding' is for professional determination.

■ In the case of directions imposed within a full Supervision Order, it is for the court to determine. However, even a competent child's refusal can be overruled as described above.

Appendix 2: Confidentiality & Contraception

■ All doctors' patients (including those aged less than 16) have a general right to confidentiality.

■ In very rare cases e.g. if a doctor believes that a young person is being abused/exploited and is unable to persuade that young person to permit confidentiality to be relaxed, s/he should tell the young person of her/his intentions and inform the relevant agencies.

■ A doctor is entitled to give contraceptive advice or treatment to those of less than 16 **if**:

• The young person understands the doctor's advice
• The doctor cannot persuade the young person to inform her/his parent/s or allow the doctor to do so
• The young person is very likely to begin or continue having intercourse with or without contraceptive treatment
• The young person's physical and/or mental health are likely to suffer without advice/treatment
• The young person's best interests require the doctor to give advice and/or treatment without parental consent

NB. The above criteria are known as the Fraser guidelines.

■ Where a doctor decides **not** to respond to a young person's request, s/he does not have to inform parent/s.

■ The doctor should encourage the young person to inform, or allow the doctor to inform, the parent/s.

■ In the case of a young person, subject of a Care Order to a local authority, parental responsibility is shared by that local authority with the young person's parent/s.

■ If such a young person does not satisfy all the Fraser Guidelines criteria listed above (which would legitimise accepting the young person's consent only), then lawful consent can be provided by either a parent who has parental responsibility or the relevant local authority.

■ Unless to do so would place the young person at risk from the parent/s, the local authority which is told that such a young person is receiving contraceptive advice and/or treatment would usually inform them.

Appendix 3: CAE Publications

From CAE Ltd Pantiles Langham Road Robertsbridge East Sussex TN32 5EP tel: 01580 880243 email: *childact@ dial.pipex.com* or order via our secure on-line facility at *www.caeuk.org*

- Children Act 1989 in The Context of Human Rights Act 1998
- Children Act 2004
- Child Protection
- 'How Old Do I Have To Be?' (a simple guide to the rights and responsibilities of 0–21 year olds)
- Sexual Offences Act 2003
- Children & Young Persons Act 2008
- Safeguarding Vulnerable Groups Act 2006
- Assessment of Special Educational Needs
- Criminal Justice & Immigration Act 2008
- Mental Capacity Act 2005
- The Children (Scotland) Act 1995 in The Context of the Human Rights Act 1998

www.caeuk.org
Discounts on orders of 50 or more of any one title

Subject Index

Notes

Notes

Notes

Notes

Notes